Copyright & Thanks

ISBN: 978-1-3999-6807-2

© Copyright Ann-Marie Jones and Justin Jones. The authors retain moral copyright over this work.

All rights reserved. Without limiting the rights under copyright reserved above, no part of this publication may be reproduced, stored or introduced into a retrieval system, or transmitted in any form or by any means (electronic, mechanical, photocopying, recording or otherwise), without the prior written permission of both the copyright owner and the publisher of this book.

The Lightning Process® is owned by and registered to Phil Parker PhD. Thank you, Phil, for your valuable feedback.
For more information, see https://lightningprocess.com/.

Thank you to Paul McKenna's team for their help. For more information on Paul McKenna's great work, see https://www.paulmckenna.com/.

The beautiful cover was created by Hayley Jackson Designs https://www.hayleyjacksondesigns.co.uk/ . She's a gem!

Thank you to Jane Finch at https://www.time4inclusion.co.uk/ for reviewing the inclusivity of this book. Jane really knows her stuff! There's always more that could be done, but the book is significantly more inclusive as a result of our work together.

All images are those of the authors or have been lawfully purchased. All works remain copyright of their original creators.

We have tried to credit all original authors whose work has been referenced. If we have missed anything, please email us at prettydarnfast@gmail.com and appropriate accreditation will be provided in a future revision.

The authors cannot take responsibility for any action or inaction you or anyone else takes. If unsure, please contact a qualified professional, such as your doctor.

Thank you to Dee J and Tina F, for your incredible help. Hey Jazzy!

Pages of Happiness

Copyright and Thanks...1
Introduction 3
Changing Old Habits 18
Making Positive Choices... 46
Dealing With Heightened Feelings 60
Quiet Mind... 70
Rest... 138
Sleep 152
Confident, Organised & Positive... 164
Further Reading 192

Introduction

IMPORTANT

> **Do not read this book until you are ready to change**

This book contains hypnotic techniques.

Do not try them if you have epilepsy, are driving, or operating machinery.

This book is not intended as a substitute for medical care.

If in doubt, please consult your doctor.

Our best efforts have been made to make this book as inclusive as possible.

To help all readers, text in this book is **not justified**.

This book uses British English spelling (e.g. 'color' will be written as 'colour').

Your Spirit Horse

Imagine, deep inside of you, a horse that's your inner spirit. It's a **beautiful creature, powerful and strong**.

Now, **currently your horse may be saddled with weights**. It may be trudging through the day. It may resent the fences of the field and is **not seeing the beauty around** it. It certainly isn't standing proud.

In this book, we are going to **teach it how to lose those weights**, how to see the beauty of the field, and maybe give it the confidence to **jump the fence**, if that's what it wishes.

With some effort, we'll have removed enough bags that it can tackle the final few itself, or accept what it has and **run freely** anyway.

I don't know if you've seen the **joy and freedom** of horses frolicking in a field, but it's a delight to see. **Your horse is capable of having this.**

Share The Love

This book has taken many hundreds of hours to write. **The only purpose of this book is to help you**.

Providing you with the best possible information in a compact, fun, and colourful way has always been at the top of our priority list.

If you find any of the information of use to you (or even just a picture you like!), please head to Amazon and post a 5 star review.

We're using Amazon's 'Print on Demand', so we can't check the print quality of each book ourselves. If you're not happy, please review the book based on the content rather than the print. We hope it's as beautiful as we intended.

If you feel this book is anything other than 5 stars, please email us at prettydarnfast@gmail.com and tell us how we could improve. Please forgive us a typo or two - we've done our very best! This is personal, not business, so if you get in touch, please allow us a little time to get back to you.

Thank you and happy reading.

Can You Trust This Book?

We've taken the **finest wisdom from the finest minds** - from the oldest of sages to the very latest research.

We've found modern magic from Paul McKenna, Eckhart Tolle, Phil Parker, Michael Neill, The 14th Dalai Lama and many more.

We've gone back thousands of years to when people started working out how to live a happy life.

It's amazing - from **Africa to America, Asia to Europe, many similar themes arise**.

If you want 100% proof, feel free to read the thousands of pages of books and watch hundreds of hours of videos and attend all the learning sessions that we've done.

Alternatively, you can get a 'quick start' by reading this book. We've taken tons of that **gold-standard stuff** and fitted it neatly into fewer than **200 beautiful pages.**

This book is just about the fastest way to help you get a life you will love.

In case you're wondering, there is no 'upsell' in this book. Isn't that nice to know! Anything we recommend is of pure belief and we won't receive a penny from anything we recommend in this book.

Positivity

This book includes themes around being positive.

Having a more positive outlook doesn't mean being happy all the time. It's not motivational posters or faddy hashtags. It's not about ignoring emotions.

Having a more positive outlook will help you approach your situation in a more productive way. According to the Mayo Clinic (a respected resource), benefits from having a positive outlook include:

- Increased life span
- Lower levels of distress and pain
- Greater resistance to illness
- Stronger recovery from illness (even serious illness)
- Better psychological and physical wellbeing
- Better coping skills
- And a whole lot more

This book includes validated techniques for you to enjoy a more relaxed, happier life. Positivity is part of that.

Contradictions

This book includes some contradictions.

It includes the work of many different people. As such, we've included different views and approaches.

For example, hypnotherapy and Neuro Linguistic Programming (NLP) may look at ego strengthening. Mindfulness may focus on letting go of your ego altogether.

It's up to you which to choose. You might even decide on a bit of both and use the different techniques in different situations.

Incidentally, the 'no ego' philosophy is the reason there's not an 'About The Authors' section to this book. This book isn't about us. It's about you.

The only thing that matters is that you find something of use to you.

**FOR FASTEST RESULTS
READ SLOWLY**

Will This Work?

You're reading this book because you want to **improve your situation.**

You probably already know that to get good at something you have to practice. As well as reading this book carefully, **do the exercises and keep practicing every day, because it will lead to a better life.**

Don't just take our word for it. Try it. See for yourself. It might just be the **start of something great**!

You made a really positive step in getting this book, so make the most of it and **continue that good intention**.

Can I Change?

As we learn, our brain makes links. These links get stronger the more we use them.

When you were young, you learned to move around. To start it was hard, but the more you did it, the easier it got. The brain **strengthened those links until you didn't even need to think about it**. It took practice, but you did it!

Later in life you started forming beliefs. Can you think of a time you believed something that turned out to be wrong? We've all been wrong at some point! So if you have doubts about whether you can change, that's fine. With practice, you'll soon see how those old ways can change - and maybe faster than you expected.

You can imagine the following exercise if needed:

1. Draw a line from the starting arrow. When you get to a decision point, choose to finish at the 'Happy Relaxed Cat'.

2. Do this 5 more times.

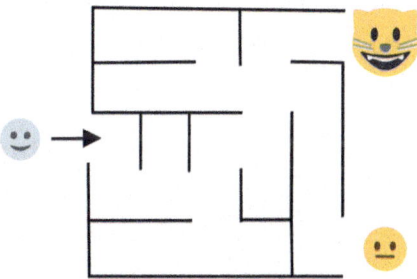

See how strong those links are looking now! That's what we are going to do in this book.

Practice

Have you noticed how **the more you practice something, the better you get**?

The more you do something, the stronger those neurons in your brain fire, often to the point you don't even need to think about it any longer.

Have you noticed how, **when you stop practicing, you get a bit rusty**, sometimes forgetting completely?

In this book, we will identify bad habits, stop them, and replace them with new, better habits.

We don't tackle individual issues because, if we fix a specific problem, you'll just find something else to worry about.

Addressing mindset provides the resiliency and confidence to find your own solutions and get a life you will love.

Learn positive habits. Create stronger links. Lead a better life.

If you aim at nothing, you hit nothing.

Take Aim!

The Tale of Two Wolves

An old Cherokee is teaching his grandson about life.

A fight between two wolves lives within all of us.

One is evil – it is anger, envy, sorrow, regret, greed, jealousy, arrogance, self-pity, guilt, resentment, inferiority, lies, false pride, superiority, and ego.

The other is good – it is joy, peace, love, hope, serenity, humility, kindness, benevolence, empathy, generosity, truth, compassion, and faith.

Which one wins, asks the boy?

The One You Feed

Changing Old Habits

Gems from The Lightning Process®, plus wisdom from sages old and new.

If you want different results, you have to do something differently

Anxiety And Stress

Thousands of years ago, we humans **evolved a system for keeping us safe** from wild animals that might harm us.

The human body can only do so many things at once. It has limited resources.

So, when a threat is present, it **shuts down some important functions** to deal with the immediate problem.

Specifically, it shuts down:

- Complex thinking
- Digestion
- Sleep management
- The immune system

The brain cannot tell the difference between real and imagined threats (really!). So, when you are overthinking, anxious, stressed or worried, it manages the shutdown for whatever this phantom threat might be.

So continual stress is affecting you more than you realize.

Let's Tackle Anxiety, Stress, Guilt And Unhappiness

Anxiety, Stress, Guilt and Unhappiness can feel like strong emotions, but they **are fundamentally fragile**.

They work using similar patterns almost like a set of ingredients.

If you think of a cake, **changing just one ingredient can fundamentally change the cake**.

That's what we'll do here. See which ingredients aren't great, swap them out for some good ones and we are on our way to more positive times!

The best time to make those changes is RIGHT NOW.

You Are A Genius!

Genius: Exceptional intellectual, creative or natural ability.

Are you aware that you are, in fact, a genius?

By existing as a human at this time, **you have the most amazing brain ever made**.

If your brain were a computer, it could store over THREE MILLION movies!

And you've used it to consistently provide great results on demand, unconsciously and automatically, every day!

By being able to read this, you've shown you can teach your brain something the rest of the animal kingdom can't manage and you do it without even thinking. Genius!

Many of us slip in a bad habit or two. By repeating, we unintentionally become a genius at those as well.

Now, the great thing about the human mind, is that while it can feel in control, actually, **you are in control**. You can program it to do whatever you want, just like you programmed it to read!

Have you noticed how easy it can be to fail at something, or to forget?

Great. Because that's what we'll harness. **We are going to 'fail and forget' the bad habits, and replace them with new joyful ones** that will lead you to a life you'll love.

Filtering

Your mind is fantastically efficient. One of the ways it gains efficiency is by **focusing on what it needs** and not paying so much attention to the rest.

When you read this book, you are probably not seeing the rest of the room in detail. Yes, your eyes are focusing, but your mind is choosing what to focus on.

Exercise

Quickly look at the image below for a few seconds. Look for all the **RED** (red) triangles, then cover the image.

How many red triangles did you notice?

Filtering (Continued)

Now, without looking back, how many **BLUE** (blue) circles can you remember? What about **GREEN** (green) squares?

Can you remember as many of these shapes as the red triangles?

Most likely you picked out the red triangles quite strongly, even though **they were the least common object**!

Filtering is essential for survival, but over-focusing on the negative aspects of life can result in missing the many lovely things around.

If you are looking for negativity, you'll find it.

The great thing is that **you can turn this around. Once you start looking for positives, you'll notice more of them** and the negatives will fade into the background**.**

Turn Bad Filters

Bad filters see:

- How dangerous and scary everything is
- Things we should worry about
- Evidence of unhappiness
- The way we get things wrong
- How success was the result of someone else's action
- How embarrassing our errors look in front of other people

Exception filter:

- Things are going so well, it must be the calm before the storm.

Into Good Filters!

Instead look for:

- **All the times things go well** (even little things)
- All the things working just fine without your worry or control
- The ways in which **you are lucky and supported**
- How you mostly get things right
- How **successes were at least partly as a result of your actions**
- How people aren't concerned or even aware of your errors, so generally it doesn't matter. NOBODY gets things right all the time. To err is human.

Exception filter:

- When things *aren't* going so well, it's just a blip. It won't last and good times are ahead.

Take Bad Generalisations

Bad generalizations usually include absolute terms like:

- Every time
- Always
- Never
- Nothing
- As usual
- Nobody
- All

Examples:

- I never get it right
- Every time I stop worrying, something bad always happens
- I have to control everything
- Nothing ever works

And Prove Them Wrong!

When you use such phrases:

Raise an eyebrow and ASK

REALLY?

Every time?
Always?
Never?
Nothing?
As usual?
Nobody?
All?

Then take time to consider if that statement was really true?

Think of a time it wasn't and notice how these generalisations are so easily proved to be false.

Revel in disproving them!

Imagined Past/ Futures

Bad things are often in the past or an imagined future

Past

- I should have done

Future

- Might all go wrong

What matters is getting out of our imagination and being in the Now.

Being In The Now

The past and the future don't exist.

You can't touch them or feel them. **They are just figments of your imagination.**

Your past memories are skewed by your interpretations and the future cannot be predicted.

What matters is NOW. This very instant.

- What you can see
- What you can hear
- What you can feel

As it's so important, we will explore more on this later in the book.

Identify Negative Soundtracks

Negative soundtracks follow the pattern:

- What if? [imagined future]
- How will I cope?
- I can't cope
- Not again
- Why?

And Do The Opposite!

With even more conviction and authority than the doubt:

- **It will go amazingly.** Imagine how great it will go and how easily you will deal with any issues.

- **I know I will cope.** I have done in the past and I'm still here (and/or because I am strong).

- **I am coping.** Deep down, I am strong.

- This is just another blip before things get better again.

Yes, these are skewed, but are they really any more skewed than the negative soundtracks?

And which version is more pleasant to live with?

Turn Overdrive

Overdrive looks like:

- Keeping busy
- Always on the go
- Rushing
- Not taking breaks between tasks

Into Neutral

- Mindfulness
- Meditation
- Relaxation
- Fun
- Time with pets
- Chatting casually with friends & family
- Taking time over meals
- Changing your posture

Allow yourself 'time to be'.

Allow yourself to drop the ball once in a while.

Your busyness may seem important now, but it's most likely that in a month's time you'll have forgotten why you were busy and realise it wasn't that important after all.

Stepping Back

This technique can be used for **mild** irritations.

1. Think back to a time that was mildly upsetting. Maybe an argument, disagreement, or somebody offended you. Imagine the scene as you experienced it.

2. Now, freeze that image in your mind, so everything is completely still.

3. Imagine yourself stepping out of the image, so it's like you're looking at a picture of that scene.

4. Drain the colour out of the image so it's black and white.

5. Shrink down the image until it's the size of a speck of dust.

6. Flick the speck away. It no longer matters to you.

Stepping Back Decreases Feelings

Be aware of when you do this and use it in moderation. Too much stepping back might not be a good thing.

Re-Experience Good Feelings

The more you associate with something, the stronger the feeling becomes.

If you imagine being somewhere, feeling happy and full of energy, you will get real benefits from it.

1. Think of a time you had a really good experience. A time when you felt really happy.

2. Imagine the scene in full. The more detail you can imagine, the stronger the feelings will be. What did you see, hear and smell? How did you feel at that exact moment?

3. Now make the colours richer, brighter and bolder and the sounds louder. Notice what happens to how you feel.

4. Imagine yourself absorbing the good energy from this scene directly into your body. If you wish, you can give that energy a colour. So, for example, you might envisage rays of purest white light pouring directly into your body.

5. Imagine the energy concentrating in your stomach and spinning around.

6. When you're ready, let that energy spread back out to every part of your body.

Association Increases Feelings

Regaining A Sense Of Control

The feeling of 'being out of control' can seem strong, but it is the weakest of all.

If you were to imagine each negative feeling as a block in a toy tower, this feeling would be the very top.

By **taking the steps shown** previously, this 'top of the tower' feeling will **soon go away**.

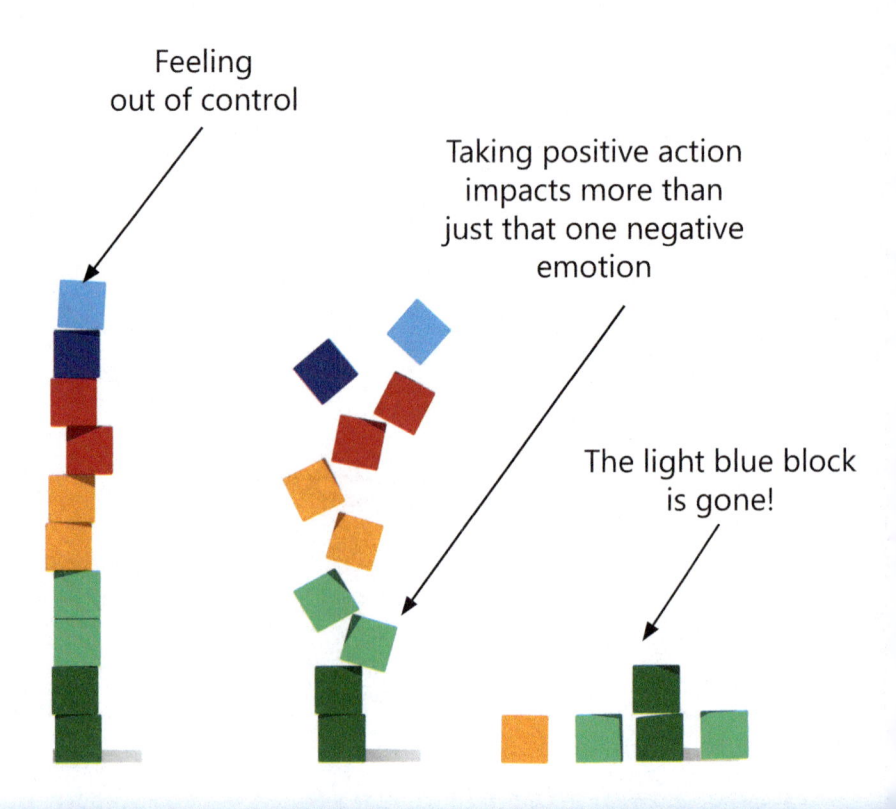

Feeling out of control

Taking positive action impacts more than just that one negative emotion

The light blue block is gone!

Guilt

A teenage girl has identical twin brothers. They are the same in almost every way.

Both the twins are very fond of chocolate (who isn't!).

One twin used to steal her chocolate, but stopped a while back. He doesn't feel guilty about what he did. He just decided to stop and is at ease with how things were.

The other twin continually steals her chocolate, but feels terribly guilty about it.

Who is the better twin right now?

Say Goodbye To 'Your Story'

In our mind, we often carry a story of 'who we are'.

This can often have negativity attached. For example: I grew up poor, I wasn't very good at sport, or I've been ill.

Your mind may use that 'past you' to provide a narrative about your identity.

In order to be truly free, you need to let go of whatever has been.

By letting go of the past, you can focus on the Now. The actual you. The you right Now.

Once the past is laid to rest, you can change your own narrative and reshape your future.

Make Your Inner Voice Friendly

Next time your inner voice is being talkative, listen and see what the voice sounds like.

Is it loud or soft? Is it quiet or harsh? Where is it in your head?

Then ask yourself, how would you like it to sound?

What if you tried to make that voice friendlier?

Try changing that voice to something you would prefer.
Maybe try a few different ones, then pick a favourite. Something that's pleasant to live with.

If the inner monologue is calm and friendly it helps ease your day.

Being Present

We often talk about 'being present' or in the 'Now', so what does that mean?

Being present is experiencing what is happening at this very instant.

It is what you see, hear, feel, smell and taste in this instant.

Anything other than that is away from the 'Now'. It is thinking, planning, remembering, stressing and worrying.

One of the most important things we can do is notice when we are NOT in the present and gently bring ourselves back to it.

This is a life long process. At times it's easy, at others, less so, but it's always beneficial to your inner self.

How Changes Over Time Work

Much of how we feel and our resilience is in our perception.

Real Life

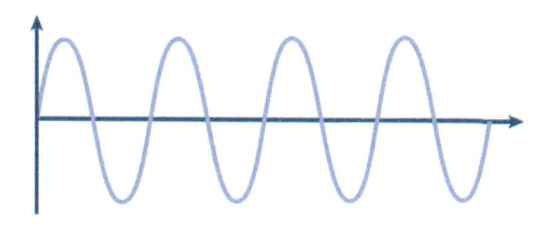

Negative Outlook

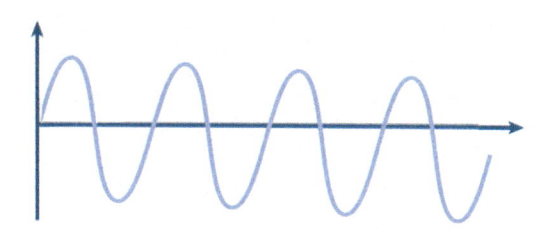

Positive Outlook

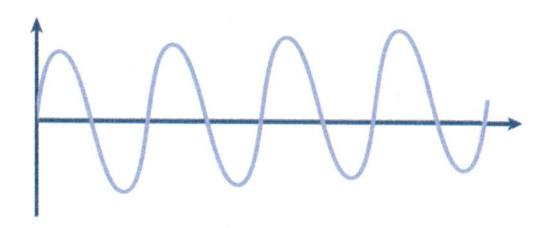

Being **positive** and seeing the bad times as just a 'blip' helps us to be **more resilient** in the rough times, and allows us to **enjoy the good times more**!

Making Positive Choices

A solution based approach using NLP and SFBT

You Have The Answers Within You

'Solution Focused Brief Therapy' (SFBT) is an approach to helping people that gets rapid results.

SFBT uses questions to help you find your own solutions. Finding your own solutions helps you become more adaptable to whatever you might face in the future.

Some interesting points to note:

1. There are probably times in the past you have solved something similar before.

2. There may well be instances of where you are already working towards, or even achieving, your desired future.

3. If you are currently going through something that feels constant, there may be (or have been) exceptions - times when it wasn't present.

4. You are already handling your situation better than you realize.

5. You might have started making small changes without noticing.

In this section, we'll look at using a little SFBT for problem solving in daily life.

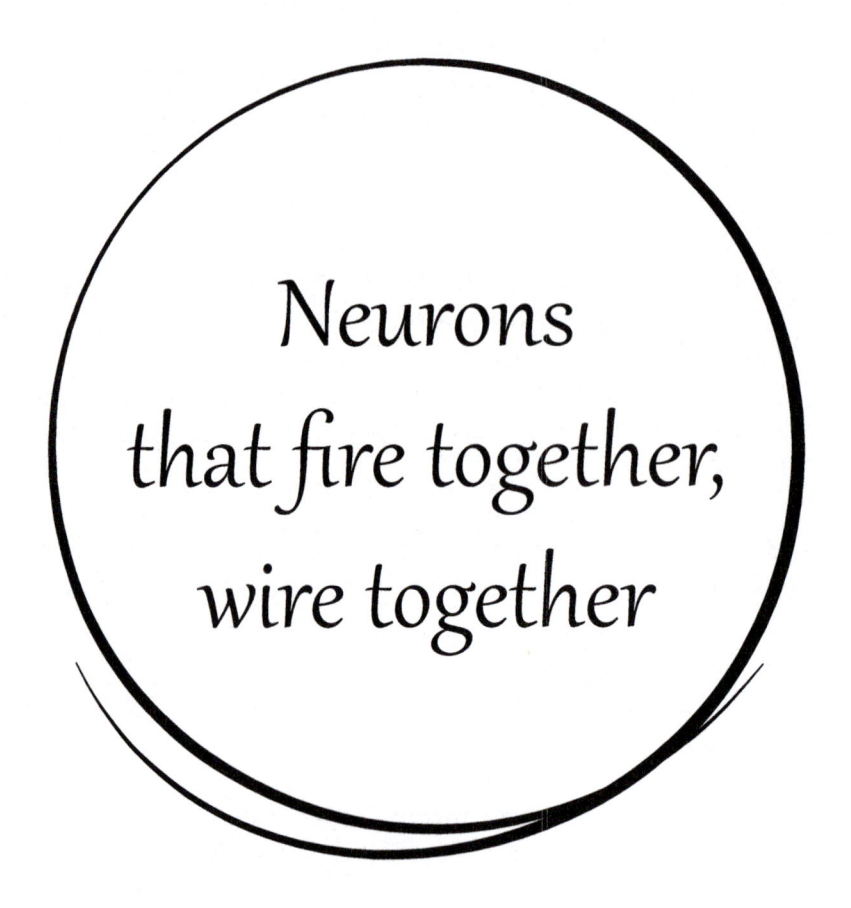

Neurons that fire together, wire together

Using Hebb's Law - Momentum Of Change!

"Neurons that fire together, wire together"

Your brain makes associations all the time to save time and energy.

You probably already know about Pavlov's Dogs. By ringing a bell at meal time, he trained the dogs to expect food whenever they heard a bell.

In many ways, we are just the same.

Examples:

- Turning on the radio when you get in the car
- A feeling when you hear a certain song
- Getting your phone out when you're on the loo

By using the following process repeatedly we can become automatic at instilling positive change.

1. Notice

The first rule of holes is: '**If you find yourself in one, stop digging**'.

Most people pay attention to the 'stop digging' part of this phrase but, actually, noticing you're in a hole is just as important. Without noticing, how can you change your behaviour?

If you've noticed you're not having any fun, feeling stressed, anxious, overthinking, overwhelmed, or anything else negative; great!

Yes, that's right, great! You've just found something that could be improved and now the good bit can start!

When you do this, congratulate yourself.

You've just started the process of change.

2. Label

Once you've noticed something that's not optimal, the next step is to label it.

By labelling, you step out of the problem and enable yourself to change.

You are no longer 'in the problem'. You are the conscious observer.

You can choose your own label. The key is to **say it calmly**.

Use **just one word.**

For example, you might calmly say to yourself "anxiety", "stress", or "overthinking".

3. Fork In The Road

Hypnotherapy sometimes places a person at a fork in the road. This creates a more visual path to change.

**Do I want to go left (continue),
or right (find a more positive path)?**

Have you noticed anything that could be considered a 'right fork' action so far in this book?

As you read on, you might find many more.

Focus On The Road Ahead

A quick game:

Don't think about pink penguins.

Can you do this without thinking, at least a little, about pink penguins?

In order to not think about something, you actually have to think about it to then decide not to think about it. The focus is actually on the thing you're trying not to think about.

Put another way, if you were getting a taxi (cab), you wouldn't say "I don't want to be here". You would instead say something like "I'd like to go to the swimming pool please".

This is why, **from now on, the focus is all about where you're going**.

4. The Right Path

Try these two questions in order:

A. What is my positive goal right now?

A positive goal must **focus on the desired state**, not the thing you don't want. It must have concrete, observable actions and, ideally, be detailed.

For example:

- I want to have a more enjoyable day at work.

- I want to have a calmer day today, as I catch up on my tasks.

B. How can I make it happen?

- It must be deliverable by you. You can't expect to change other people.

- It must be reasonable.

Examples

- I am going to take time to chat to people at the water cooler, and do breathing exercises to stay relaxed.
- I am going to make a list to prioritise my tasks for the day, then focus on each task in turn and not worry about the others.

Example

You're lining up for a parking space when someone cuts in, steals the spot and looks at you as if to say 'what are you going to do about it?'.

You're about to react.

Actions:

1. **Notice the change in your mood**
2. **Calmly label it, if you wish**
3. **Pick a path (choose positive change, of course)**
4. **What is my positive goal right now?**

To enjoy my day regardless of this person.

How can I make that happen?

- I am going to step back from the problem. It's just a parking space. It really doesn't matter. I might smile to myself as I consider how silly it would be to get het up over such an insignificant thing.

- I'm going to take a slow, deep breath (or a few), and calmly move on to find another space.

This might seem like being passive or weak, but it's actually a case of *'softness overcoming hardness'*. I wish to go about my day in harmony. This will get me what I want.

Feelings Of Urgency

When feelings of urgency arise, consider doing the following:

1. Notice the urgency
2. Step Back
3. Slow down

When we feel urgency, our brain starts to race.

Research consistently shows that when a person's mind is racing, they miss details and make rash decisions.

For example, if someone annoys you, your sense of urgency may want to address the issue immediately.

However, taking a little time to cool off (and maybe some deep breaths) will bring some clarity to the situation.

Does it matter? How can you present your thoughts in a way that makes your point, while keeping things cordial?

This can also work well when someone is being urgent with you.

Taking time to slow down and step back may help to see: Is it really that urgent? Is there another way that makes things easier? Could something else be bumped to avoid a build up of priorities?

Calm is contagious, so your calm approach will also help others around you.

57

Delay Your Worries

Ideally, you will deal with things as they arise. **Sometimes though, things may take a bit more thinking about.**

If this is the case:

1. **Set a time when you will think about them.** For example - if it's homework related, you don't need to think about it until the time you set aside for homework. If it's work stuff, you only need to think about that during work time. You're not being paid to think about it outside work time!

   For more general things, you may want to set a time of the day **(not just before bed).**

   This is also good because it means your brain will be working on the problem in the background while you're back to having fun.

   Make sure there's a defined end time to any handling session! If you can't complete the task in one session, book another time slot and get back on with enjoying life.

2. When a thought or worry arises, **write it down**. Acknowledge it. **You are now free to stop thinking about it until the set time.** It's written down, so it won't be forgotten.

3. Practice all the good things in this book until that time for action.

At the appropriate time:

1. Figure out what's at the root of your worry.

2. Replace worries with truths.

   I may be worried about tomorrow's presentation, but I've done presentations before and I'm still here. And now I'm more experienced, so I know what to do.

3. Figure out what's in your control. You can't expect to change other people.

4. Change how you feel, or take action, or do both.

Dealing With Heightened Feelings

Identifying

When you identify with, or over-focus on something, you increase your bond with it.

As we saw previously, stepping back and reducing focus on a single element makes room for a happier, more diverse life.

It's important to remember that you are many things.

If you have an illness - you are not that illness.

If, for example, you have asthma. Don't think of yourself as 'asthmatic', but just as a person. That person may or may not be experiencing asthma symptoms right now.

If you are afraid of spiders, don't think of yourself as 'arachnophobic', but as a person. If there are no spiders around right now, you are just a person.

Go Towards Your Fears

Irrational fears are **often born from an unintentional action or avoidance**.

A common one is a fear of large kitchen knives.

An avoidance mindset might look like:

I didn't use the big kitchen knife. I was safe. Therefore the right thing to do was not use it.

But of course, you could have used it and been completely safe too.

The action to take

If you are scared of the big kitchen knife, consider using it when preparing your next meal.

Notice how no harm comes from it. Notice how the care you naturally take makes it safe to use. Notice how it's making your job easier than using the little blunt knife.

The more you do this, the more comfortable you'll become.

Positive Imaginations

The brain can't tell the difference between real and imagined events.

You can use this to your advantage, by **imagining an event and dealing with it effortlessly.** This trains your mind to relax in a 'been there, done that' kind of way.

Racing drivers imagine a race over and over before they start. By the time of the race, they already know the corners and the best passing points, because they've envisaged doing it over and over in their mind.

Exercise

Scenario: You have something coming up that you are uncertain of.

1. Find a place where you can close your eyes without distraction.

2. Imagine you at the start of the event. You are feeling confident and relaxed. See what you would see, hear what you would hear, feel what you would feel.

3. Now, imagine the event happening. Keep seeing, hearing and feeling. Imagine how you deal with any uncertainty effortlessly. Imagine performing at your very best and notice how great that feels.

Do this multiple times for best effects.

The Fear (Or Success!) Ladder

If you have a fear of something and can't get straight past it, you can always build up.

Just like breaking a large journey into 'stops' (with treats!), achievement is much easier when you break it down.

Take fear of dogs for example. It's reasonable to be a little cautious of dogs you don't know, but most dogs are very friendly. Maybe with help from a friend, or someone you know, you could try using a ladder like the one below.

Step	Activity	Fear Level
1	Looking at photo's of dogs	2
2	Watching a film with dogs in	2
3	Looking at a dog through a window	3
4	Being in an open area where there's a dog on a leash	3
5	Standing near a sedate dog on a leash	4
6	Standing beside, but not touching a dog on a leash	5
7	Petting a very sedate/old dog on a leash.	6
8	Petting a sedate dog off a leash	7
9	Petting a younger dog on a leash	8
10	Petting a more active dog off a leash.	8

NOTE: You may see these ladders drawn the other way around, but this way makes for a better reading flow.

Nudging (A True Story)

A builder in his 20's went to see a therapist. His problem? He wore underwear just once, then binned them..... Really!

Seven brand new pairs of undies a week. Buy, use, bin.

The therapist *didn't* try getting to the root of the problem. She didn't spend hours getting him to talk. She just asked one thing of him.

Wear your undies twice and see how it goes.

Buy, use, wash, use, bin.

This would save him half his money and everything would still be nice and clean, right? He agreed to give it a shot.

As you might have guessed, once he got used to that little change of wearing washed underwear, and experienced the joy of having more money, the cycle was broken. 2 wears quickly became 3, 4 and more. He was free, saved a lot of money (and helped the planet too!).

If we have an unusual habit, we may want to 'just be normal' and find the answer straight away. But often, just changing a little thing can break the cycle and help us get exactly what we want.

The Havening Technique

1. Think of a mildly upsetting time, or something that makes you feel mildly anxious. Give that feeling a rating of 1-10, with 1 being the lowest and 10 being the most intense.

2. Now, clear your mind. Stroke your forehead and cheeks 10 times.

3. Cross your arms over your chest. Start stroking (repeatedly) from your shoulders down to your elbows. Close your eyes.

4. Still stroking, imagine walking in a pure beautiful meadow and count out loud from 1 to 20.

5. Open your eyes and calmly say out loud 'calm and relaxed' three times.

6. Close your eyes again.

7. Still stroking, imagine slowly walking down a luxurious staircase and count 20 footsteps.

8. Open your eyes.

9. Rate how you're feeling from 1-10. If you're feeling better, great. If you need more time, you can repeat this as often as you like.

Hypnosis

If the brain is like a computer, then **hypnosis is like uploading new software** to that computer.

A good hypnotist can really help you calm down your nerves and get you in a better position to address a situation.

If you're short on time or money, there are lots of resources online. Many therapists make recordings you can make use of.

The chances of having an issue that's unique to you are very slim.

Just like with teachers at school, some therapists you'll click with, others maybe less so, but the practice itself is sound and very effective.

If you were to pick just one resource to go further with hypnosis, **'Freedom From Anxiety', by Paul McKenna** is brilliant.

Hypnosis has been proven to work using sign language. If required, a good hypnotist may be able to work with a sign language interpreter to help.

Quiet Mind

Finding peace and serenity

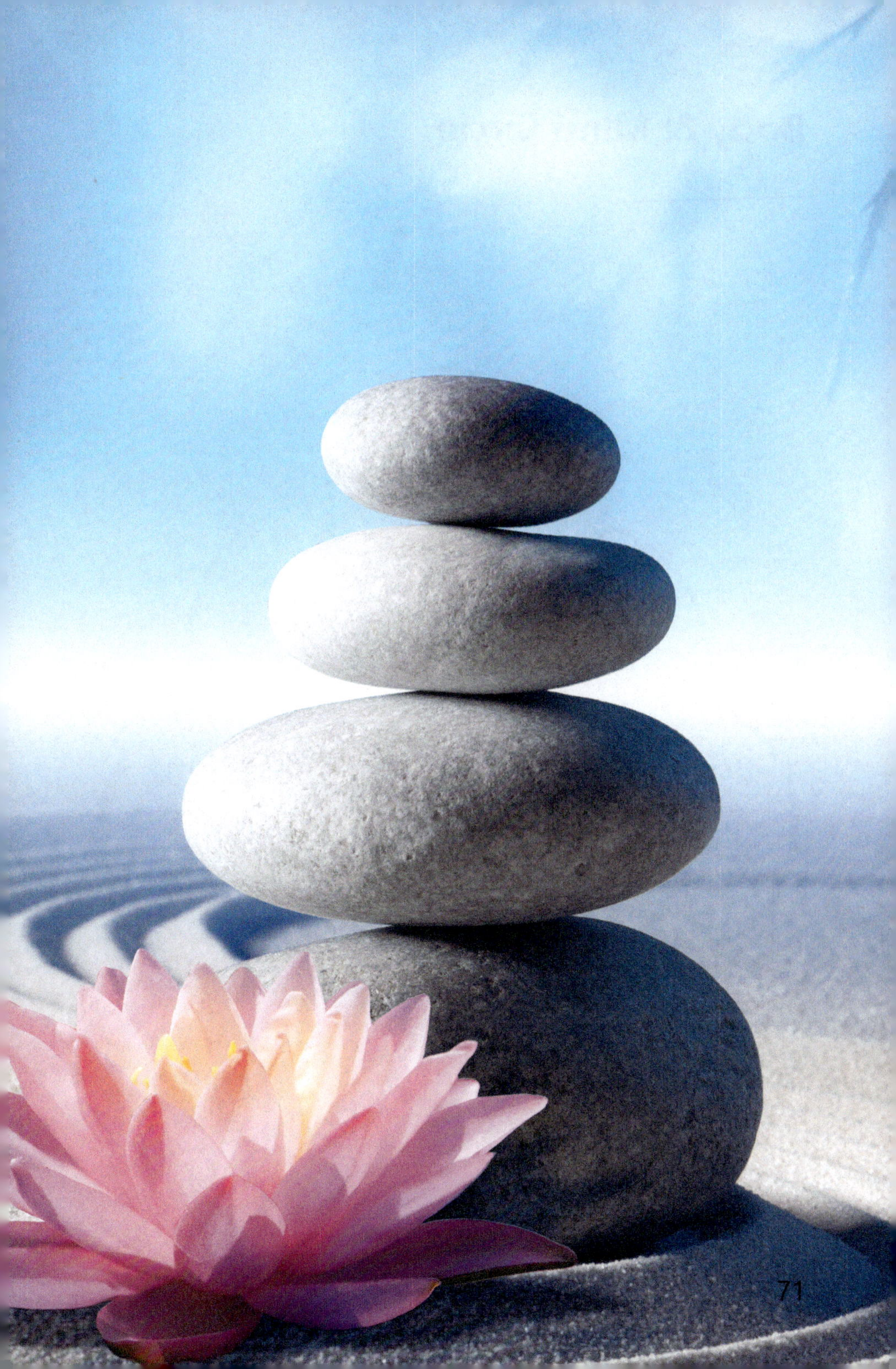

Body & Mind Circle

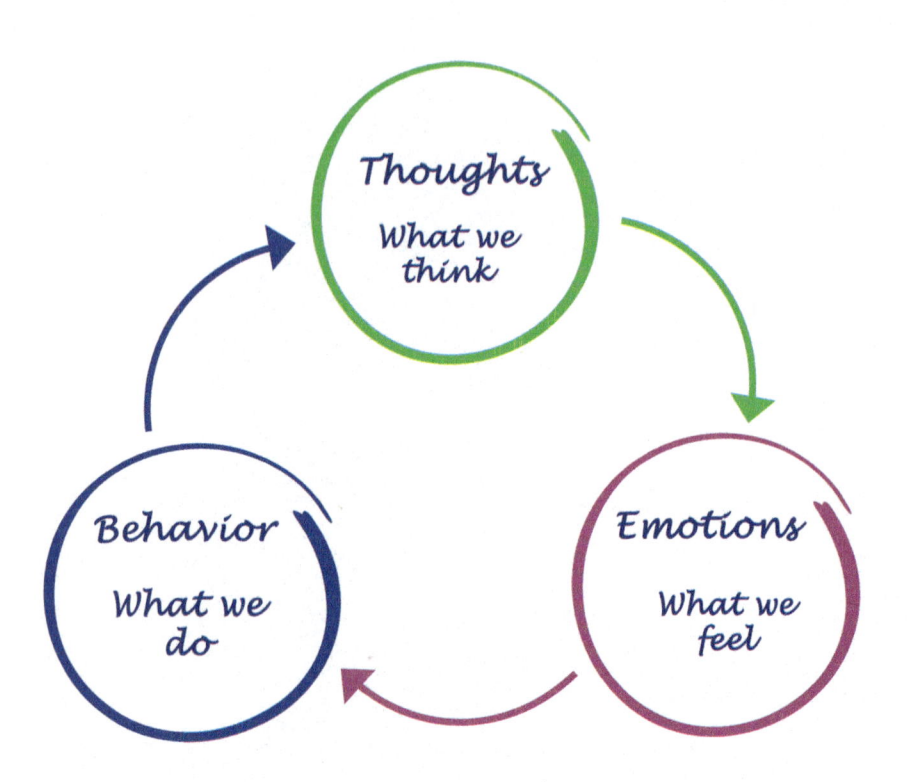

- **Thoughts** — What we think
- **Emotions** — What we feel
- **Behavior** — What we do

Our thoughts affect our emotions.

Our emotions affect our behaviour.

Our behaviours affect our thoughts.

By actively thinking more positively, we can change how we feel. Example: Seeing a bad event as part of the ups and downs of life means we feel more at ease.

By taking better charge of our emotions, we can improve our behaviour. Example: Stopping a snap reaction gives us time to respond in a more reasoned way.

By changing our behaviour, we can change our thoughts. Example: By practicing mindfulness, we can enjoy calmer thoughts.

A change made at any stage will magnify its effects all around.

Simply changing your body posture can make you feel more confident. Feeling more confident, you behave more confidently. A virtuous cycle manifests.

Interpretation

The way we interpret the world makes a huge difference to how we react.

Albert Ellis defined this as the A,B,C Model of Emotions.

- A. The situation itself
- B. Interpretation (the running story in our mind, which we often take as fact)
- C. Reactions (our impulses to act)

We often think that a situation aroused our emotions, but often it's our interpretation of that event.

The commentary in our mind is often very strong and we fail to separate that from what's really happening.

It's why two people can be at the same place at the same time and have two very different experiences.

Read the following sentences, one by one. Try to cover the sentences below the one you're reading.

Pause at the end of each and imagine the scene as best you can.

Steve was walking to school.

He was anxious about the science class.

He hoped he could keep the class in better order this time.

The teachers were on strike, so as a parent, he felt it was his duty to help out where possible.

Our mind is always working to interpret the events. Did you notice how it changed as information became available?

A whole story is never available to us. When someone bumps into us and gets angry, we don't know the day they've had or why their impulsion is so strong. We can, however, choose how we interpret and react to that person.

The Mind Camera

We think we see the world like a camera, accurately recording what's in front of us.

However, **our mind actually translates information from all the senses**.

So, what we 'see' is actually more like an artists painting, or a map. Some parts are simplified, some parts are made more pronounced. To some parts, we attach meaning.

Take the first image on the next page. Do you see an apple, or two people facing each other? With an open mind, you may be able to see both.

Now, looking at the second image, do you see a white triangle in the middle, even though the lines aren't there?

Everything your senses process are interpreted by your brain.

Everyone's interpretation is unique.

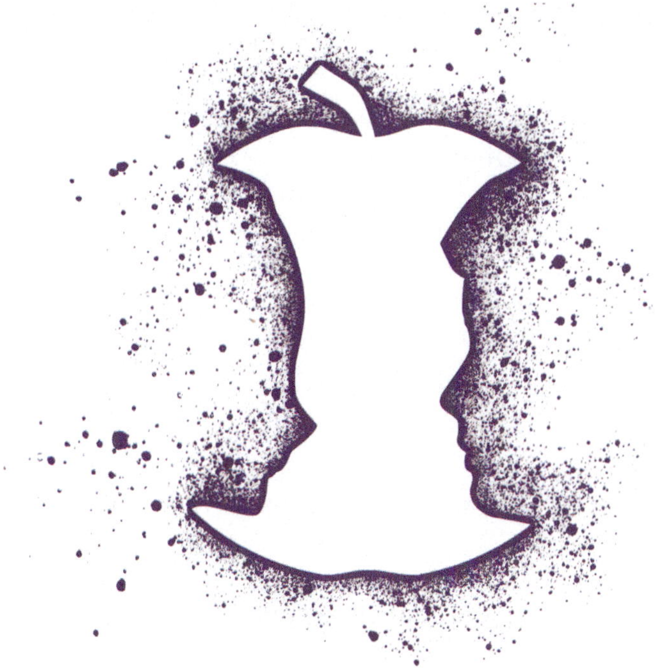

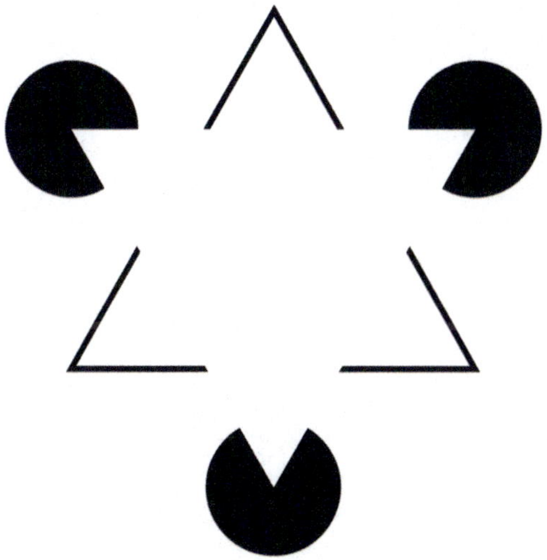

Mindfulness

Mindfulness is a **scientifically validated** technique to help you enjoy moments of inner peace.

The best things about it are:

1. It's **FREE**

2. **You can do it anywhere**, at any time, no matter what your ability

3. It's both **relaxing and helps you be more alert**

A busy mind uses a lot of energy. Mindfulness helps restore the balance.

Here, we'll explore some ways in which you can practice mindfulness.

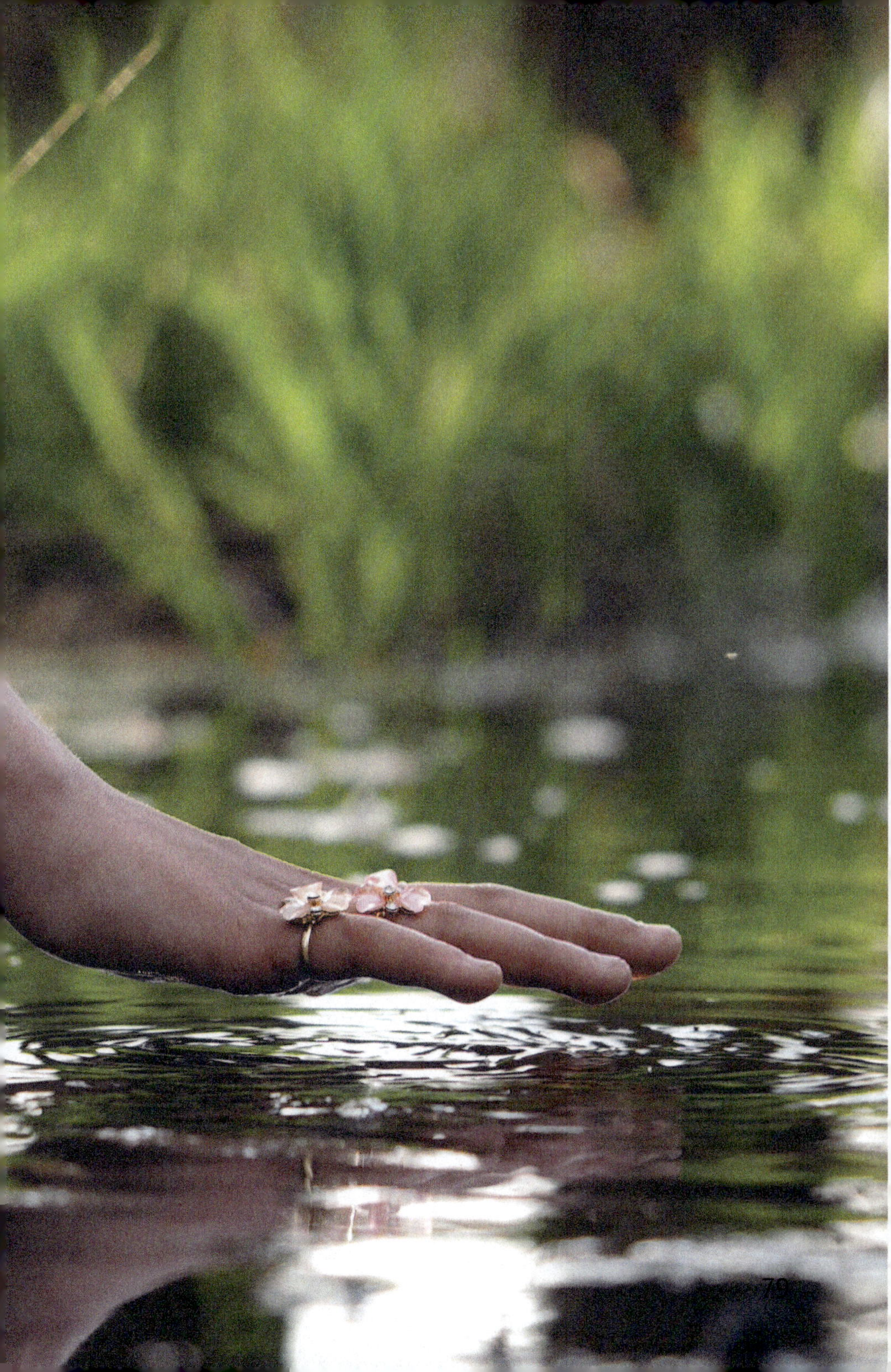

How To Practice Mindfulness

Mindfulness is:

Using your senses to notice what's happening at this very moment.

When you do this, you give what you are seeing, hearing, feeling, touching and/or smelling your full attention. You do this without judgement.

The 'without judgement' part is really important. When you notice what's around you, your mind may try to categorise as 'good' or 'bad', but this is irrelevant. Gently move away from the story and back to noticing.

If you are missing senses, or certain senses require a lot of effort, use whatever is available and most comfortable for you.

Mindfulness is great when done surrounded by nature, but **it's best wherever you are right now!**

If you are reading this as an e-book, you can adapt the following exercise to your tablet or e-reader.

The next page has been intentionally left blank.

How does the page look when you really look at it? What do you notice about the texture? Does it look different in different light? How does it feel as you run your fingers over it? Does it smell? How does it sound as you turn the page?

Mindfulness - Walking Mindfully

You don't need to be in the countryside to walk mindfully. Here's a standard suburban road in Britain on a dull day. Most people wouldn't pay any attention to it. But there's so much to notice.

Are there any flowers in the grass or gardens?
What can you smell?
Can you see the house numbers as you pass?
Are the house styles all the same, or different in some way?

What are the colours in the sky? How are the clouds?
What colour are the cars?
Are the trees blossoming, or sprouting? Any birds in them?
How does the wind feel on your face and hands?

What can you hear?
Is the road surface one colour, or is it a mix? Is it even?

Every walk, even along the same street, is different.

Mindfulness - In The City

If you are walking through the city, **pay attention** to what's around you.

What's the **sky** like today? Can you feel **heat or coldness**? Can you feel a **breeze** on your hands and face?

What can you **see**? If you notice litter, **don't judge** it, just look at the colours and the patterns.

What does it **smell** like as you pass the bars, cafes and restaurants?

Can you **hear the sounds** of bikes, vehicles, animals and people?

How many people have stopped at this junction?

How many people missed the artwork on display?

Look At The Sky As Often As You Can

The sky is ever changing. Day and night, always something different to see.

Mindful Eating

How much attention do you pay to your food?

For example. Have you ever looked at toast?

Take time to notice:

- The different shades of brown, even black, in the colour
- The holes in the surface
- The sheen of the butter
- How it smells
- How it sounds when you crunch it
- How it feels as you chew

Such things can feel odd to start, but they can help slow you down, relax and enjoy what you're eating.

Washoku - Eating The Rainbow

In Japanese cuisine (Washoku), special emphasis is placed on **fresh ingredients** and **using 'the five colours'**.

These are: red, yellow, blue (green), white and black.

'Ultra-Processed Foods' (UPFs) - foods that contain more than five ingredients - are commonly available in the shops.

However, Ultra Processed Foods lower brain function and are linked to many health issues.

By getting back to eating fresh, non-processed food, you can really help your body and mind be at its' very best.

Leafy greens are an excellent source of 'prebiotics' and will do wonders for your tum!

Eating Slowly - Asian/ Spanish Style

Eating slowly aids digestion and helps with a more relaxed style of life.

If you're wolfing down food with a fork, why not try changing to chopsticks? If you can't use chopsticks, there are lots of free resources online to show you how.

The Spanish and Portuguese cultures have really mastered slow eating with Tapas and Petiscos. **Sharing food around and chatting** while you eat makes meal times much more pleasant. It helps your digestive system too.

After Meal Walks - Italian Style

La Passeggiata is the Italian word for **taking a leisurely stroll after dinner**. These walks are often quite social, reconnecting with family and neighbours after a long day.

Taking **several short walks** throughout the day is **better for you than one big walk** at the end of the day. It's been shown to increase your body's handling of blood sugar as well as numerous other benefits.

Wanting A More Natural Life

For well over 2,500 years, humans have been wary of current technologies and wanted to get back to something 'more natural'.

When exactly should this time be?

- Back to when many humans perished in harsh winters?
- When a 100 mile journey took days?
- Before hospitals and sanitation?
- Before you could speak to a distant friend/relative?
- When finding the answer to a simple question took weeks?

Technology is just Earth's elements in a different form.

We shouldn't fear it. We should look how it can improve our lives and use it for good.

If you find something that could be better, maybe your calling is to make it so?

News

The news can be pretty rough at times.

Is this because the world is bad? Nope!

Is it because calm and serenity are considered too boring for ratings - Absolutely!

Consider these headlines:

- Little girl reads with her mum before bed
- Young boy kicks a ball for the first time
- Local road pothole fixed
- Kids doing above average at local school
- Person nurtures 2 hives of bees

Lovely and completely boring (in the eyes of the media)!

News companies need you hooked. They need eyes for adverts or to justify their existence. Tension gets this.

Ask yourself - Is the article I'm reading sensationalist, or trying to feed on negativity? Could I access news in a more factual, less emotive way?

You could try taking a bit of time off from the news - see if it makes any difference. Maybe use the time you've saved to do something positive.

Money Worries

'Super Coach' Michael Neill wondered - what's the magic number where you stop worrying about money?

Then, in his coaching role, he had a client with £600 million in the bank and still worried!

It became clear - no such number exists.

When Alexander the Great asked what he could do for Diogenes (who lived in poverty), Diogenes asked only that Alexander step out of his light, so he could enjoy the sun.

While it's undoubtedly harder if you're struggling to pay the bills, it's important to remember that how we feel about money is just the result of thoughts.

Feelings of security will come and go regardless of our bank balance.

The Backwards Law

The more we strive for something, the more difficult it is to obtain.

For example, in the words of Alan Watt - 'Insecurity is the result of trying to be secure.'

Being overly clingy to a partner causes them to want space.

Trying to be positive all the time leads to frustration that nobody can feel as such.

Have you ever tried to solve a problem, got stuck, then found the answer magically arrived when you were doing something else?

Our unconscious brain is more powerful than our conscious brain. We can trust it to find solutions without trying.

Sometimes the best thing you can do is 'do nothing'.

Turn The Volume Down

1. Listen to the voice in your head. How does it sound? Is it loud? What is the tone of the voice?

2. Imagine you have a volume knob and this controls the volume of the voice.

3. Now, imagine turning the volume down. Turn it all the way down until you hear only silence.

4. If the sound is more stubborn, actually try turning the volume up (just a little). If you can do that, you have all the power you need to turn it down. Then, turn it down.

5. You can use this technique whenever you want some peace from your inner voice. It can be an effective way of creating a moment of serenity.

The Past

The past dies every moment. It ceases to exist.

You don't need it.

Humans learn all through life and your experiences have been logged by your subconscious memory to help make you stronger and more resilient.

Only refer to the past when it's absolutely necessary to the present and ignore old negative stories.

All we really have is the NOW.

The Now is what you can:

- See
- Hear
- Feel
- Smell
- Taste

If your mind is running through stories of the past (or imagined futures), notice that you are doing so.

You may wish to label it 'thinking'. Calmly thank your mind and gently return to the present.

Everything Changes

Mount Everest seems constant, but it's always changing.

Seventy million years ago it was yet to be.

Now, it's growing around four millimeters a year, while also being eroded by water, ice and wind.

In a few million years, it will cease to exist, as the tectonic plates continue their constant change.

But, we can enjoy it for what it is right now.

You may feel like the same you, but you are different too. Every day, your body replaces three hundred billion cells.

Even your brain cells are changing, so what you were is not who you are now, and not who you will be.

Living Life

An ancient king approached his council of sages.

He wanted a simple guiding principle.

Something to bring humility in times of hubris, yet also comfort in times of need.

After thinking, the sages provided him with a ring.

On the ring was an inscription.

The inscription read:

This too shall pass

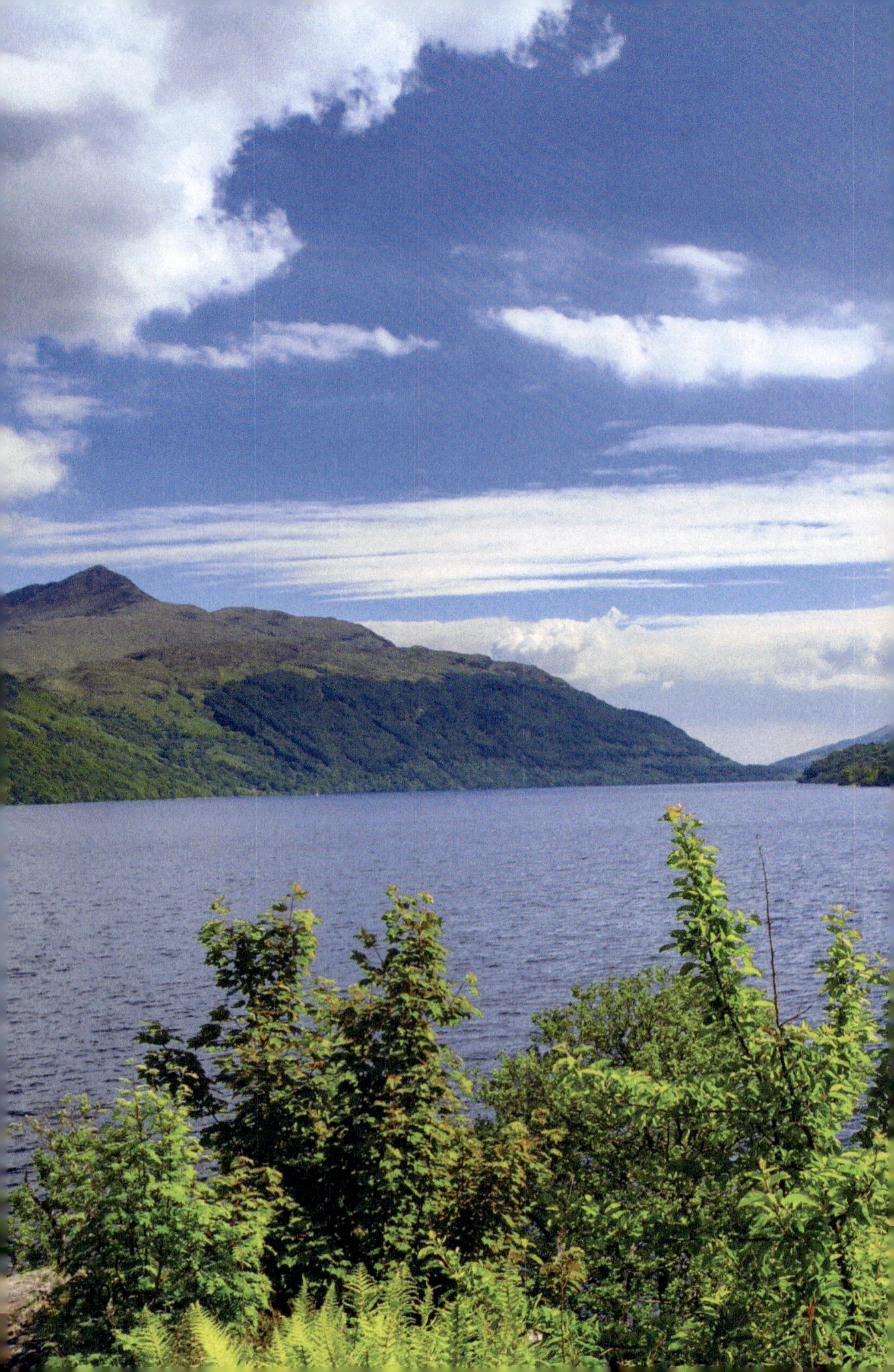

The Deep Lake

The surface of the lake may be choppy. It may be pushed about by the winds and hit by rain storms. It may shimmer in the golden sun.

But at the bottom is stillness. Unaffected by the goings on at the top.

The same stillness lies deep within all of us.

Past & Future

An exercise to re-imagine old memories. Read through first.

1. Find a comfortable position and start to relax. Slow your breathing and close your eyes.

2. Imagine a timeline, with the past behind you and the future in front. Float up above it so you can see it all.

3. See your memories in that timeline. Remember that all experiences were making you stronger and preparing you for a better future. Notice the lessons you learned.

4. Now, go to the very best times in your life. Really go deep into reliving the joy of those moments when you felt at your very happiest. If you can't remember, make something up and make it wonderful.

5. Give that glorious feeling a colour.

6. Imagine a can of spray paint in that colour. Take that can and spray it all over any bad memories. Really soak them in that glorious, most happy of feelings. Notice that looking at this colour everywhere, you feel completely at peace with what has been. You can leave the past where it is now. You no longer need it.

7. Now, think about your future. Imagine it raining with that colour and know your future is going to be full of great memories.

8. Gently return to the present, feeling relaxed and happy.

What Is Meditation? What's The Point?

Meditation is a practice that involves **focusing or clearing your mind** using a combination of mental and physical techniques.

Unlike film stereotypes, it's not about trying to reach some enlightened state. It's just a practice of finding moments of stillness - and anyone can do it.

Meditation is scientifically proven to reduce anxiety and depression, improve your ability to think clearly and help you be more resilient to life's challenges.

In this section, we'll look into different meditation options so you can find the best fit.

The Right Way To Meditate?

There is no right or wrong way to meditate.

If you are listening to a 'guided meditation' and it says to sit, **you don't have to sit.** You are perfectly welcome to lie down, stand, hang upside down - do whatever you like.

The key is to be comfortable and able to focus, with as little distraction as possible.

Take time to work out what's best for you.

If you are deaf or hard of hearing, meditation apps might not be ideal. However, meditation existed thousands of years before apps were invented, so there are plenty of other ways to get started.

Feel free to adapt the meditation exercises in this book to meet your needs.

Meditation Apps

Meditation apps provide '**guided meditation**'. In guided meditation, a teacher/speaker will calmly talk you through the process of a meditation.

There's lots of choice, so you can find your favourite teacher and whatever topic would most suit you at the time.

Calm

https://www.calm.com/ is a fantastic app. It's fairly cheap to subscribe. The 'Daily Calm' (10 mins) has lovely wisdom and is a great break from the day. Use the app for the best experience.

Simple Habit

https://simplehabit.com has some great FREE meditations and paid courses to help you learn how to meditate by yourself. You can also filter by time, which is really handy.

Insight Timer

https://insighttimer.com/ has tons of FREE meditations, and has many different teachers.

Both the app and the website are easy to use. Use the search box for what you want. E.g. (Sleep, Relax, Stress Relief, Anxiety Relief) and it will have plenty of options.

Find Meditation Boring?

The monkey mind likes to be busy. If you're feeling bored, that's completely fine.

Treat yourself with kindness and **gently bring your attention back** to the practice.

Meditation is called a practice. There is no end goal. The aim is just to practice.

If you're using an app, **it helps to find a teacher you like**, so try a few and see who suits you best!

If you find sessions too long, consider starting with 1 or 2 minutes and **build up**.

You may not finish a meditation feeling like you're magically changed, but each session builds a little relief and nourishment for your body.

Yoga / Pilates / Body Balance

Yoga originates from India. The benefits for body and mind have been known for thousands of years.

There are now types of Yoga to suit everyone, from sitting/ laying to highly intense forms, for those who like to be very active.

Hatha yoga is most common. It has quite a relaxed pace. Other varieties such as Ashtanga are great if you want to build strength and keep on the move.

Pilates and Body Balance are built on Yoga and can be quite demanding.

You can find many resources on YouTube, and local clubs are friendly and inviting to all.

Tai Chi

Tai Chi is the 'Supreme Ultimate' martial art. Its origins date back thousands of years in both natures health movement (Qigong) and martial arts used by families to protect their towns.

If you struggle to stay still, this 'moving meditation' may be more your thing.

Unlike yoga, its forms are upright, making it more suited if you have issues with your stomach or balance.

There are different styles. You may have seen (the more peaceful) 'Yang style' before. 'Chen style' is much more vigorous and 'Push Hands' practice is very involved.

For those who love to learn, it will provide endless interest.

Unlike gym exercises that usually isolate body parts, Tai Chi works on many body parts at the same time.

As such, it **consistently rates as one of the best forms of exercise, especially when recovering from illness.**

David Dorian Ross has many free videos on YouTube. His 'Essentials of Tai Chi and Qigong' (4.3/5 on Amazon) is a great intro. There are many classes around the country too.

The Breath

The breath is with us all our life. It may be laboured, it may be free, but it's always there. **An anchor you can rely on to be in the present.**

You can do the following exercise anywhere.

Calmly and slowly:

- **Feel the air flowing in and out of your body**
- As you feel this, feel your inner energy

All that you ever have to cope with in life is in this very moment.

If you are ever waiting in a queue or waiting for a friend, find the breath and observe your surroundings in that present moment.

When you breathe in, try counting to 7, when you breathe out try counting to 11.

The Body Scan

Ask: What's going on inside me?

Focus on each body part in turn.

Move from your toes, lower legs, knees, and each body part up to the top of your head.

Not thinking about the body part, but feeling the sensations.

- Is there tension?
- Is there pain?
- Is there peace?
- Is there resistance?

Don't judge what you find - just become the observer. Curious and impartial.

If you feel pain, you may wish to observe it more closely.

When you become the watcher, you distance yourself from pain. If you really focus in, you may find it moves, or even reduces.

Don't look for peace! Accept what is without resistance and you will naturally feel more at ease.

Deep Belly Breathing (Simple)

Diaphragmatic (deep belly) breathing stimulates the parasympathetic nervous system (rest and digest).

It's a **proven technique to help you relax**.

You can do it anywhere you like and you don't need any equipment. A key point is to make the out breath longer than the in breath.

1. Find a comfy position. You can sit, stand or lay down.

2. Place one hand on your chest, and the other hand near your belly button.

3. **Breathe in** slowly through your nose (or mouth, if your nose is blocked). As you do this, **push your belly out**. Ideally, breathe in for 7 seconds.

    Feel your belly moving out. Your chest should stay around the same position.

4. **Breathe out slowly** through the mouth. As you do this, **feel your belly moving in**. Ideally, breathe out for 11 seconds.

5. Repeat for as long as you wish.

Deep Belly Breathing (Advanced)

1. Stand with your legs slightly bent. Imagine a string attached to the crown of your head holding you up.

Either leave your hands by your side or, for a workout, hold them out like you are hugging a tree.

2. Breathe in through the nose and push the belly out. Feel the air coming into your tummy and imagine it swirling around.

3. On the out breath, imagine the energy flowing up your back to the top of your head, then flowing back out. Let the tummy return to its normal position.

4. Once you are used to this, on the out breath, try imagining the energy of the breath flowing out to the rest of the body, spiralling as it goes.

Note: Images are in the style of the T'ai Chi Classics.

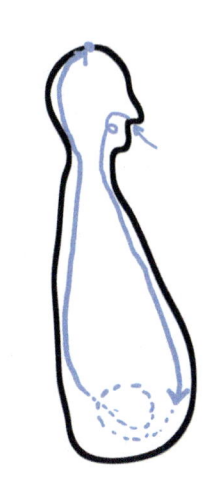

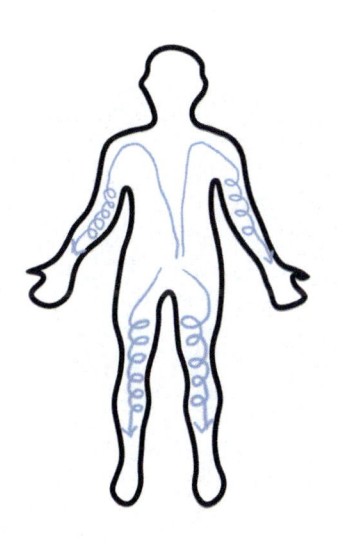

Game: I Am Transparent

At any place or time:

Imagine and feel yourself becoming transparent as if you are without the solidity of a real body.

Imagine noises pass through you.

Imagine the wind no longer hitting the wall of your body.

Imagine the light shining right through you.

Offer no resistance.

Practice in happy situations to start, then maybe try some more challenging ones.

Healing Light Meditation - Advanced

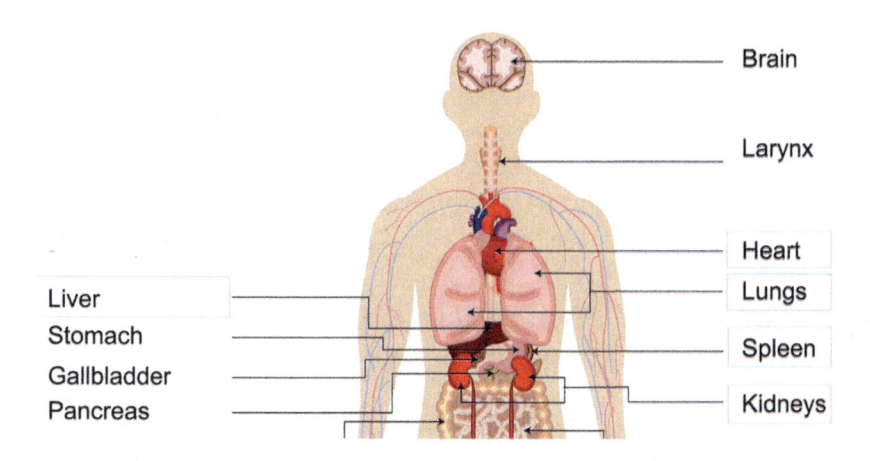

Brain
Larynx
Heart
Lungs
Spleen
Kidneys
Liver
Stomach
Gallbladder
Pancreas

Colour	Body Part	Gem
White Light	Lungs	Diamond
Red Light	Heart	Ruby
Yellow Light	Spleen	Opal
Green Light	Liver	Emerald
Blue Light	Kidneys	Sapphire

1. Make yourself comfortable, either lying, sitting, or standing, ideally with your eyes closed.

2. Using the table above, breathe in air of the imagined colour five times into the body part (or that area, if you're unsure). As you breathe in, the colour will be pure. Imagine it swirling around in that body part. As you breathe out, imagine the exhaled light darker, as if filled with impurity.

3. At the end, visualise each of the body parts shining like its' gem in the table. Lungs like diamonds, heart like ruby...

Exercise

Everyone knows that exercise is good for you. But many don't realize the benefits they can get for FREE!

A recent study found that every 2,000 steps up to 10K made a significant difference to peoples overall health and life expectancy.

Walking little and often serves your body best, so spread those steps out for maximum benefits.

To boost the benefits further, increase the pace. Surprisingly, **'brisk' (fast) walking cuts the risk of various diseases** as well as improving brain and body function. It's also much better for your bones and joints than running.

Let your mind find ways to increase your steps, whether it's parking a little further away from the shop or taking stairs instead of the escalator. Maybe just **go for a short walk if you notice you've been sat down too long**.

Cold Dips & Ice Baths

Cold showers, cold dips, plunge pools, ice baths and cold water swimming are great.

For the body, they can **decrease inflammation** and lower core body temperature.

For the mind, the shock of the cold brings you right into the present!

It feels mad, crazy and fun to do.

If you do this, **make sure you are in a safe environment**, preferably with other people around, and have warm gear for afterwards.

Consult your doctor first if you have medical issues.

Being Kind

1. On a scale of 0-10 (with 10 being the highest), how kind are you to others?

   If you're already a 10, great. Keep going!

2. If not, what could you do more of, or be more of, to make it a 10?

Ask the same questions again, but with yourself in mind.

1. On a scale of 0-10, how kind are you *to yourself*?

2. What could you do more of, or be more of, to make it a 10?

Being kind positively changes your brain. It boosts feelings of satisfaction and well-being. It gives you pleasure and even acts as a natural pain killer.

It doesn't have to be a grand gesture. Open a door for someone. Ask if anyone else wants a drink when you go to get one. It all adds up.

Kindness **increases your bond with others**, so as well as being kind, be prepared to accept kindness too. You will be helping the other person as well as yourself.

Be kind whenever possible. It is always possible. - Dalai Lama XIV

Would you treat a good friend the way you treat yourself?

The Gap

Sometimes, external noise can be really grating.

A constant whirr or drone can be easy enough to block out, but an intermittent noise can be more tricky.

Roadworks outside your house. Traffic. Neighbours doing DIY. The list goes on.

But, alongside the noise, there is always a gap somewhere.

Paying attention to the gap, and not the noise itself, can be a good way to at least make things more interesting.

Sometimes, by noticing the gap and not the noise, the noise becomes less bothersome.

Accepting what is, rather than internally fighting things you can't change, will lead to a more peaceful outlook.

Ease Critical Voices

1. Think about a time you criticised yourself or someone criticised you.

2. Listen carefully to the voice. Where it is in your head? Is it at the front? The back? Somewhere else? Notice the volume of it.

3. Now, change the voice so it sounds silly. Maybe a cartoon mouse, or another character you can't take seriously.

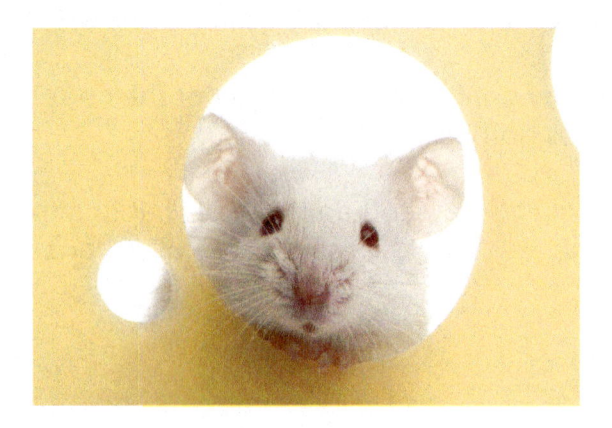

4. Change the words to meaningless, nonsensical words, like 'blah' and 'bluh'. You could even have fun making up your own replacement jibber-jabber like 'blah bluh blah, a-la-squeaken-ha'.

5. Listen to the voice again, feeling relaxed and amused now it's so foolish and powerless.

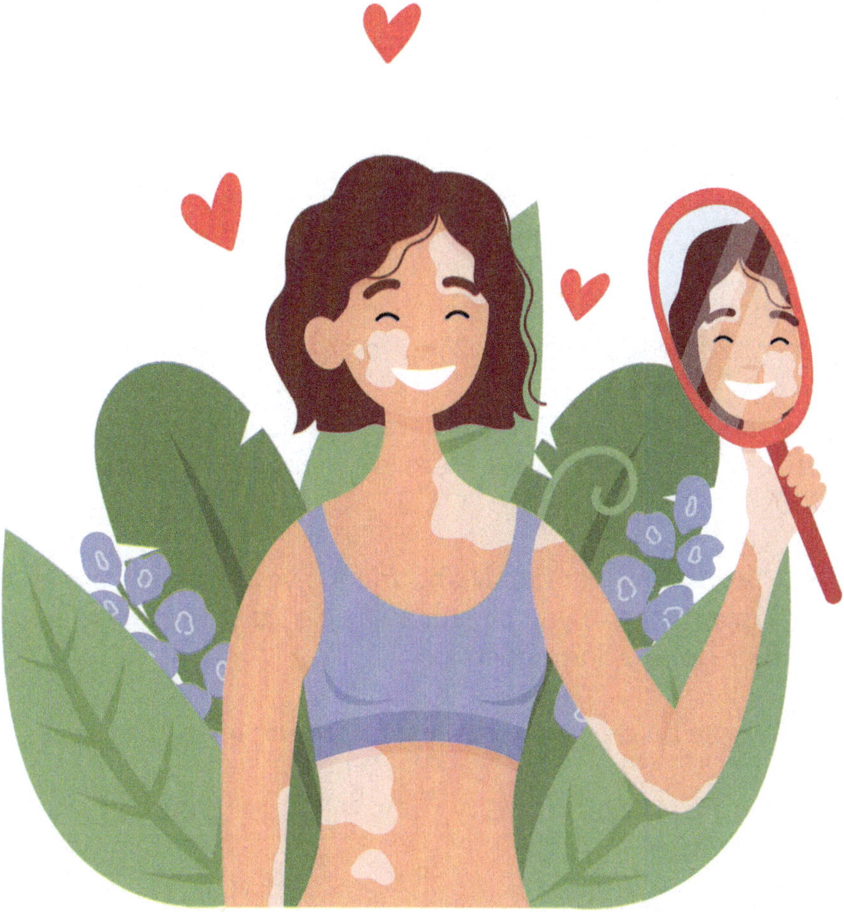

Being Sociable (In Real Life)

Over two million years. That's how long our ancestors have lived in groups!

Even as modern humans, we are hard wired to be sociable and we need to converse in person (or at least by voice) to meet that need.

This means, just as you need to be sociable - so do other people. This makes them more accepting than you expect.

As long as you have good basic hygiene and don't offend them, most people will be willing to chat.

Gyms can be tricky and anyone wearing headphones clearly wishes to be left alone, but there are plenty of other places to look.

- Making time for family and friends you already have is a good start. If you live far away, could you arrange a FaceTime/ Zoom meet?

- People on dog walks are usually friendly.

- People at sports/ hobby clubs will have shared interests.

- If you're low on funds, there are sometimes community projects to help get people together.

- Doing stuff for other people (such as a local organisation or charity) will aid socialising naturally.

125

How Much Land Does A Man Need?

Long ago, a peasant man was given a wonderful opportunity.

He could have all the land he wanted. All he had to do was walk a perimeter and return to the start. All the land within would be his.

He set out with good intentions. Enough for corn and staples for him, his wife and his children.

But when he got to the point of turning to complete the loop he thought - If I go a little further, we could have livestock. So, he went on.

With enough room for livestock, he considered how, with just a little more land, he could ensure managing comfortably even in a dry year. He went on a little more.

At the point with enough for dry years, he considered how a little more land would mean he could sell to the local village.

At each point, there was always a reason to go on a little more.

He never completed the loop.

Making Peace With Others

To help put your own mind at ease with others, here are a couple of exercises:

Hypnosis Way

1. Imagine that person. See, hear and feel them as if they are with you right now.

2. Now, freeze the image of them and convert it to black and white.

3. Shrink it down smaller and smaller until it's just a speck of dust. Then, sweep it away.

Mindfulness Way.

1. Start by breathing slowly. Try to count to 7 on the in breath and 11 on the out breath. Do this at least five times.

2. Say to yourself 3 times. I accept myself for who I am. I wish myself peace.

3. Now the harder part... Thinking of the other person, say to yourself 3 times. I accept that person. I accept them for who they are. I wish them peace.

Write It Down

The brain can only handle 5-7 bits of information at once.

If you're cluttering it with overthinking, you're not **freeing up space** to handle other information.

A simple way to clear this space is:

1. Write down whatever is on your mind.

2. Pick a time you will deal with it.

3. Say to yourself "It is written down. I don't need to think about that now"

You can put a note in your phone during the day. For late evening and night, write it on paper to save blue light from the screen waking you.

Gratitude

Gratitude is showing thanks for something. A show of appreciation.

No matter how things seem, **there is always something to be grateful for**.

The fact you can read this book, is something to be grateful for. If you have someone reading this to you, then you can be grateful for your hearing and having someone who is willing to read it to you.

You can be grateful for anything, no matter how small.

The more you notice things to be grateful for, the more you will see the good things around you.

It could be anything:

- A nice smell of coffee
- A hug
- Pretty clouds
- Something funny
- Time with family
- Time to yourself

Consider making a list of 3 things to be grateful for each day.

Reframing

If you were to take a picture of a coin, you couldn't possibly snap both sides at the same time.

Reframing is like taking a picture of the same event from a different place.

You can reframe in many ways.

Positive Reframe

1. Think of a time when things didn't go to plan.

2. Now, think of something positive that came from that event (no matter how small).

For example - I fell over and broke my thumb, but the nurse was very friendly and I got to miss a boring meeting.

The positives don't have to outweigh the negatives. It just helps to find that most events have a positive somewhere.

Time/ Context Reframe

When you are in a situation, it may feel important in that instant, but what if you change that time frame?

Expand that time over a year - does it still feel important? If you were to look back in 10 years, would you even remember it?

Experience Reframe

If you are worried about some imagined future similar to one you have experienced before, remember you have learned from your previous experiences.

You are now better prepared than ever before, and you can use your experience to help ensure you handle the situation in the best way.

Now you know about this technique, you will naturally be able to create your own reframe for any situation you meet.

Perfectionism

Does perfectionism bring you happiness and fulfillment? Or, is it a road to tire and frustration?

For thousands of years, the very finest Persian rug makers have included an imperfection. This is not the result of carelessness or accident, but is done intentionally. Intended to show that nothing but Allah (God) can be perfect.

We might think that being smarter could make us perfect. Watching the TV show 'The Chase™', we see that even The Chasers, with IQ's higher than many of us could dream of, regularly get answers wrong.

You can be greater by allowing imperfection and getting more done. For most things (probably not heart surgery!), close enough is good enough.

Ask yourself - Will I even remember this in a month's time? A year's time? Twenty years from now?

You can be greater by looking after yourself better and allowing yourself to relax.

Enjoying Imperfection

Often, we can be lulled into a perception of wanting things to be perfect.

In an otherwise great day, we have a minor disagreement or something happens that we feel tarnishes the event.

But why let that 98% of beauty and brilliance be spoiled by the 2% that isn't?

Maybe we can even learn to **embrace the imperfections**?

This singing bowl was bought with a chip in the decoration. It's a reminder that we don't have to be perfect to perform beautifully. The imperfection is part of what it is.

Carrot Cake

Luke is not a fan of the spice ginger. In fact, he'd prefer it if that spice didn't exist at all.

Now, if there's one thing that Luke likes - it's cake. His favourite is carrot cake.

Sometimes, when he buys a carrot cake, the bakers have put ginger in.

While he would rather it wasn't there, he loves carrot cake, so he knows he can put up with a bit of ginger from time to time.

Quieten The Mind

If you have racing thoughts, try this:

1. Notice the thought. Pay attention to it. Where is it exactly in your head?

2. Now, imagine wrapping that thought in a beautiful white fluffy cloud.

3. Gently float that cloud out of your head and send it off into the sky. You can send it as far away as you like.

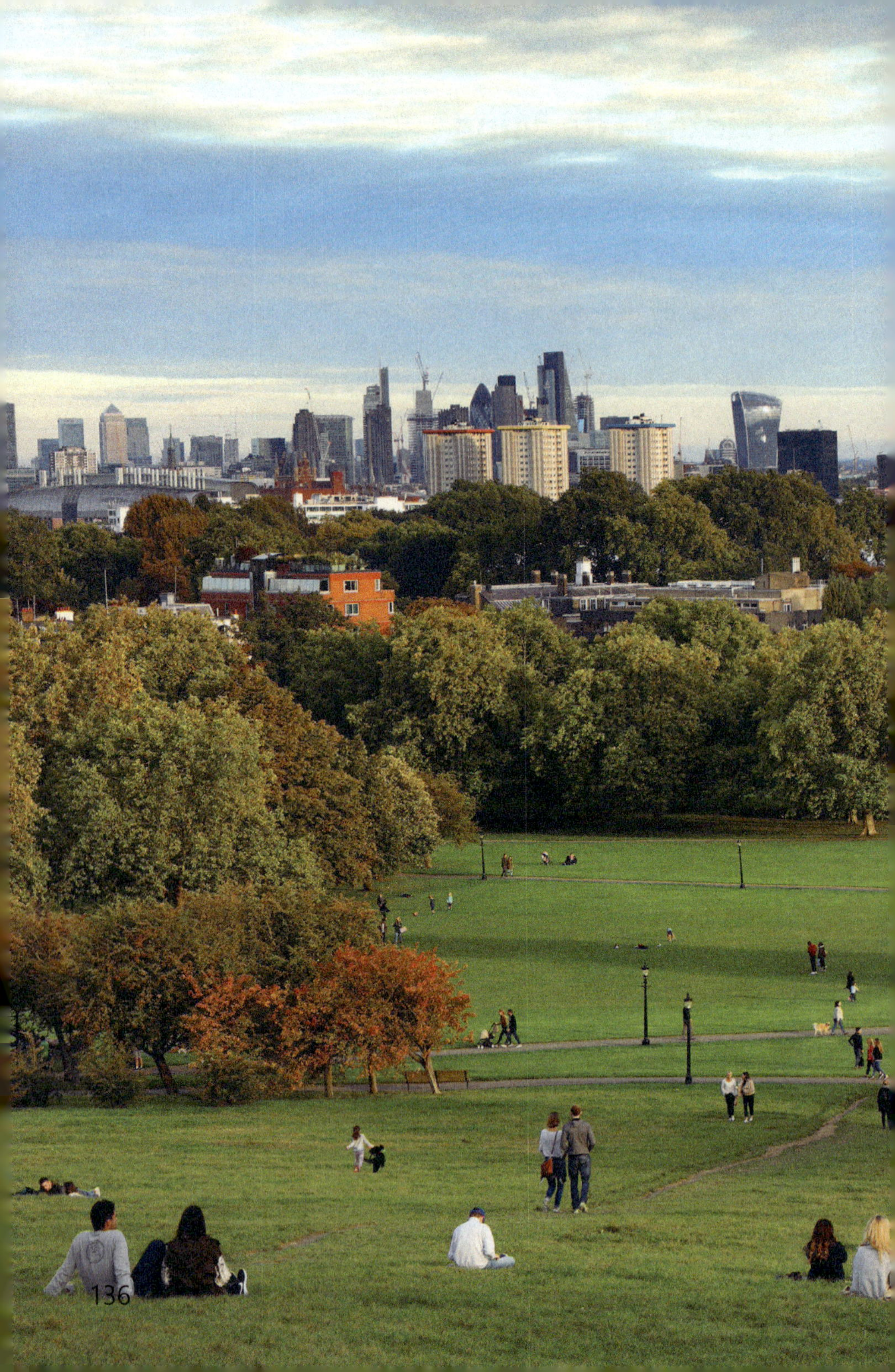

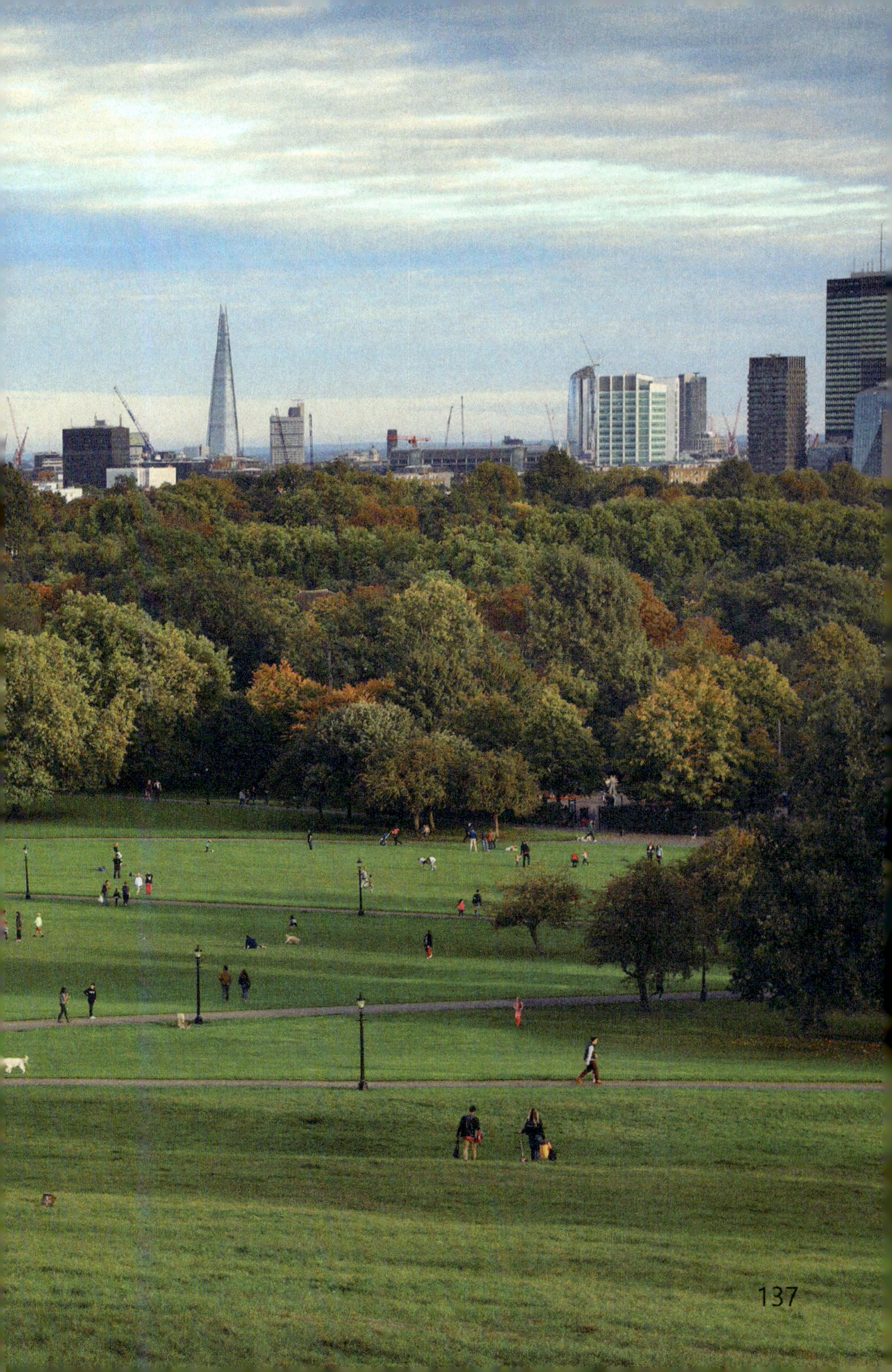

Rest

Nourishing the body

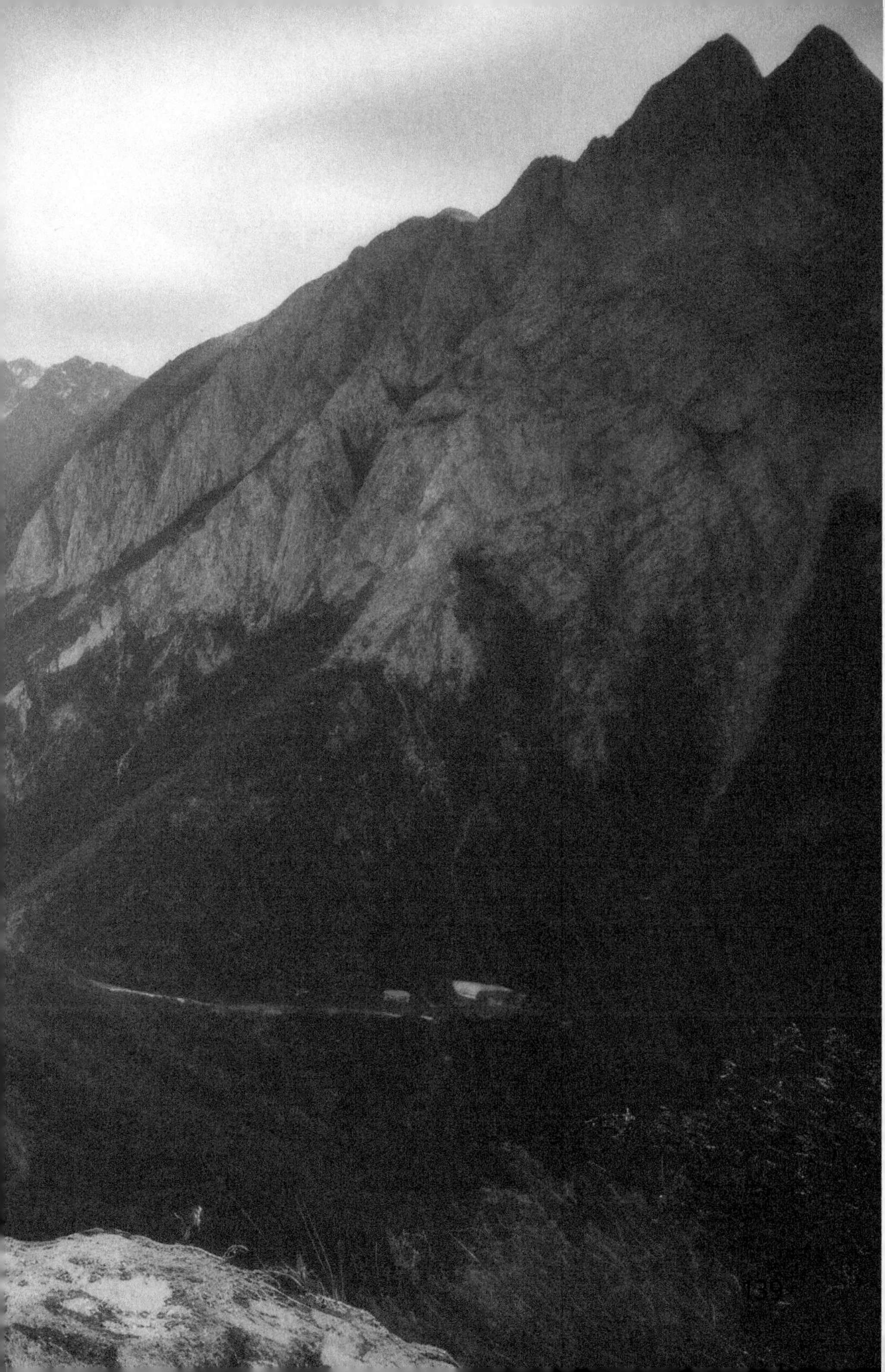

The Body Budget

The body has limited resources. It needs rest to replenish those resources.

You can think of this like a bank balance.

Things you do like work, stress, strenuous exercise and phone usage are 'taking money out of the bank'.

Things like sleep, *proper* rest, meditation and mindfulness are 'putting money back into the bank'.

Of course, we all need to take money out of the bank to function, but what happens if we don't put money in?

If we keep taking out and never putting in, we can even go overdrawn (where you owe money to the bank).

It's at this stage our body starts to break down.

If you don't take time to rest, you'll soon need time to heal.

Athletes Rest Their Bodies - Brains Need Rest Too

Rest isn't just for the body. Just like any body part, the mind needs to rest too.

If an athlete never rested, would they even make the starting line of the race?

When we are constantly thinking and doing, it's like we're an athlete who keeps sprinting and never stops.

Feeling Too Busy?

Phones are a great tool. They've revolutionised our lives.

They are a wonderful thing to own, but you can have too much of a good thing.

Are you getting your phone out regularly when you're not doing something?

How much time are you burning on social media, games, or internet research?

Phone tracking apps (such as 'Screen Time' on iOS, or 'Digital Wellbeing' on Android) will give you an honest view of your usage. You can download apps for older phones too.

Positive uses are - meditation apps, messaging friends, maps and small amounts of internet research/ shopping. Most other apps are just burning time and energy.

Studies have shown that reducing your usage by 1 hour per day will make a significant difference to your happiness.

Muting or turning off non-essential notifications can really help you forget your phone is there.

If you've cut your phone down to minimum, see what else you could cut to get even just a few minutes to yourself.

Energy Drains

Things draining a person's energy:

- Regularly binge watching programmes late into the night
- Excesses (e.g. too much time on social media or gaming)
- Stress/ anxiety/ overthinking
- Keeping busy
- Negative news
- Email
- Constantly checking your phone
- Making dramas
- Phone notifications
- Poor diet, excess sugar/ caffeine
- Clutter
- Lack of self-esteem

Notice energy drains, and try to limit their influence on your life.

Energy Gains

Things that restore a person's energy:

- Time with (good) family
- Quality time with (good) friends
- Messaging (good) friends
- Meditation
- Mindfulness
- Good sleep
- Proper rest
- Time with pets
- Prayer (if you pray)
- Positive attitude
- Enjoying simplicity
- Celebrations/ traditions/ rituals

Allow your mind to naturally find new ways to recharge.

The Restorative Power Of Nature

Spend as much time in nature as possible, whether it's a park, garden, or out in the countryside. Put your phone away. See what you can see, hear what you can hear and feel what you can feel. Let nature work its magic on you.

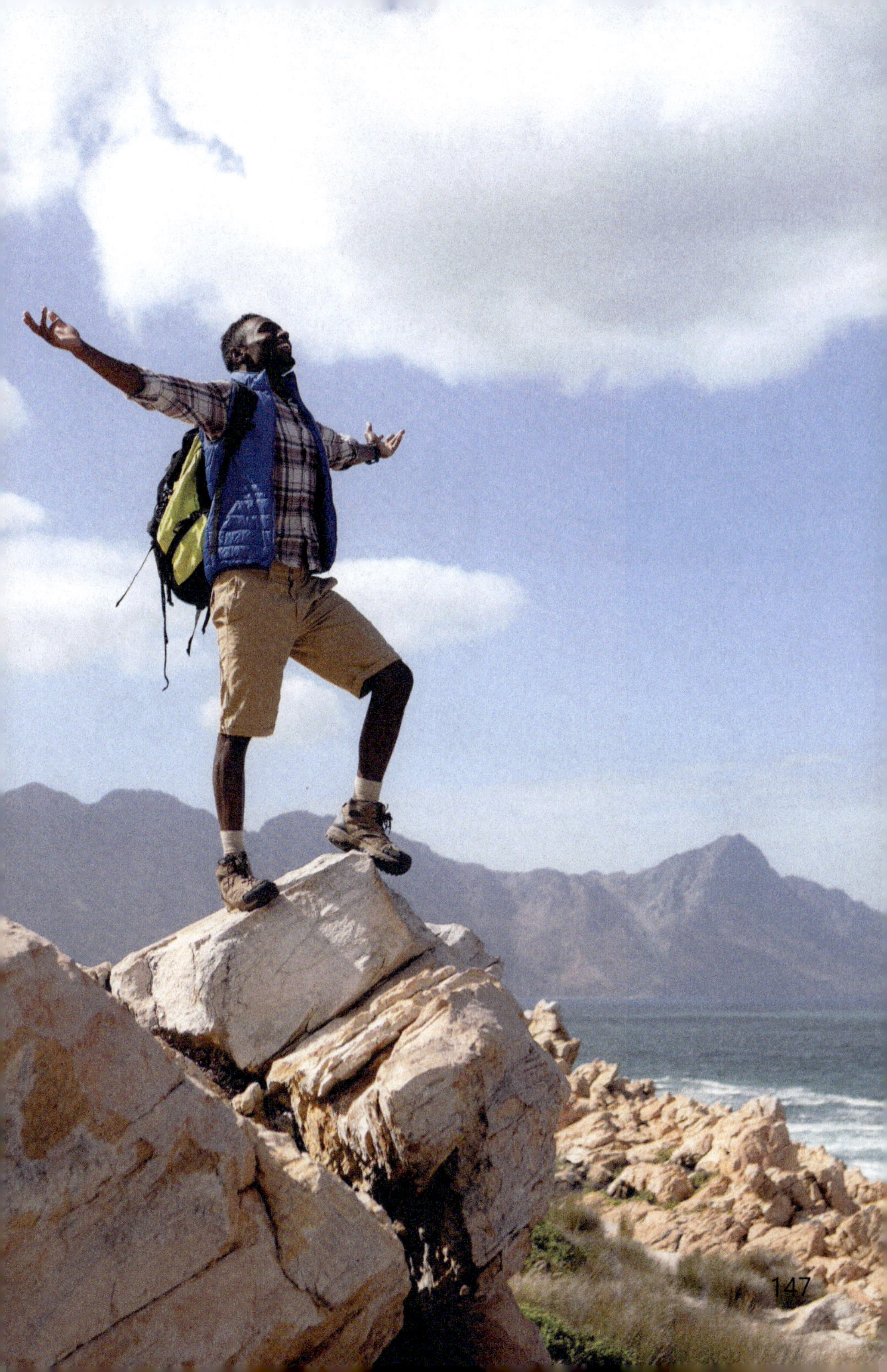

The Animal Kingdom

Have you ever noticed how animals in the wild naturally conserve their energy?

Because they don't think like humans, **they work by their body's natural requirements**.

Take the elegant lion for example.

She spends most of her days lounging around in the sun.

Then, when it's time to hunt, she's on it. Pure focus and intent. She gets her meal and eats. Then goes back to lazing around.

Be A Lion For The Day

What if you spent a day being a lion? Beautiful and full of spirit.

Take time to laze around. Do what you need to do with full focus, then go back to lazing around (proper lazing, not phone time!)

How will you feel at the end of the day? Will you feel energised and refreshed?

Napping

Napping can be great for a quick recharge, but be careful not to have it interrupt your main sleep pattern.

Regularly needing a nap could be a sign you're not getting enough good sleep, or a sign of an underlying health condition.

You may find meditation works as well as a nap and is less disruptive to your cycle.

Assuming you're not working shifts, it's best to **keep naps under twenty minutes and before 2pm** to avoid disruption to your main sleep pattern.

There are many examples of famous nappers, from Aristotle to Einstein. Einstein famously reclined in his chair with a spoon in hand and a metal plate underneath. When the spoon hit the plate, his nap was done.

Sneaky Resting

Obviously, use common sense here...

You don't have to be lying down or even on your own to take a few minutes rest.

Whether at work, school, on a lunch break, or just waiting, a person is still able to find rest.

You can always find the breath. Breathe in and feel the air coming into your body. Breathe out and feel the air moving back out. Nobody will know!

A body scan is just as subtle. What can you feel in your toes? Move to the soles of your feet, then your ankles. Move all the way up your body, feeling each body part until you get to the very top of your scalp.

It's rest and, best of all, nobody will know you're doing it.

Over time, you may be able to find other ways to sneak in a rest!

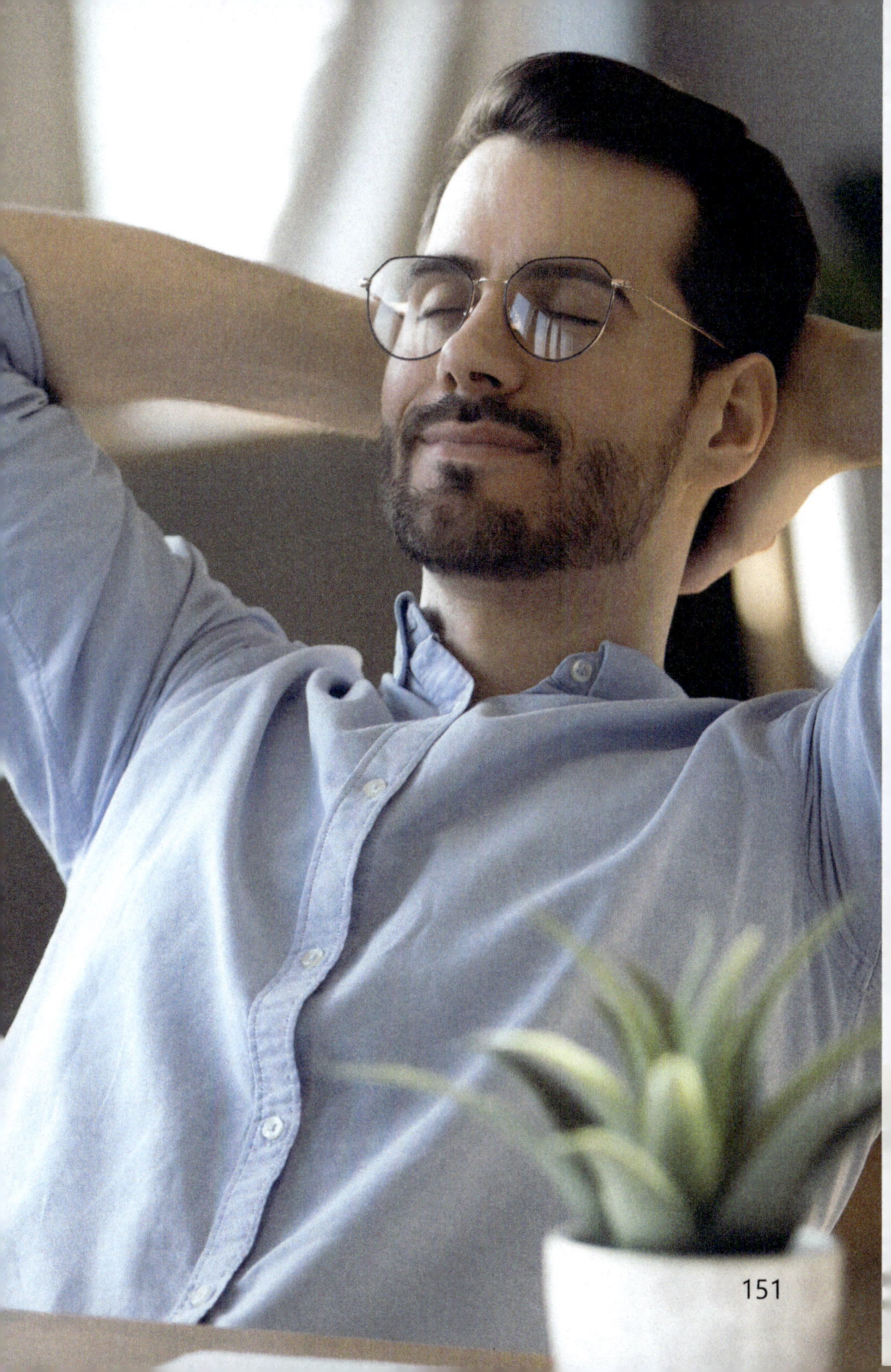

Sleep

Restoring body and mind

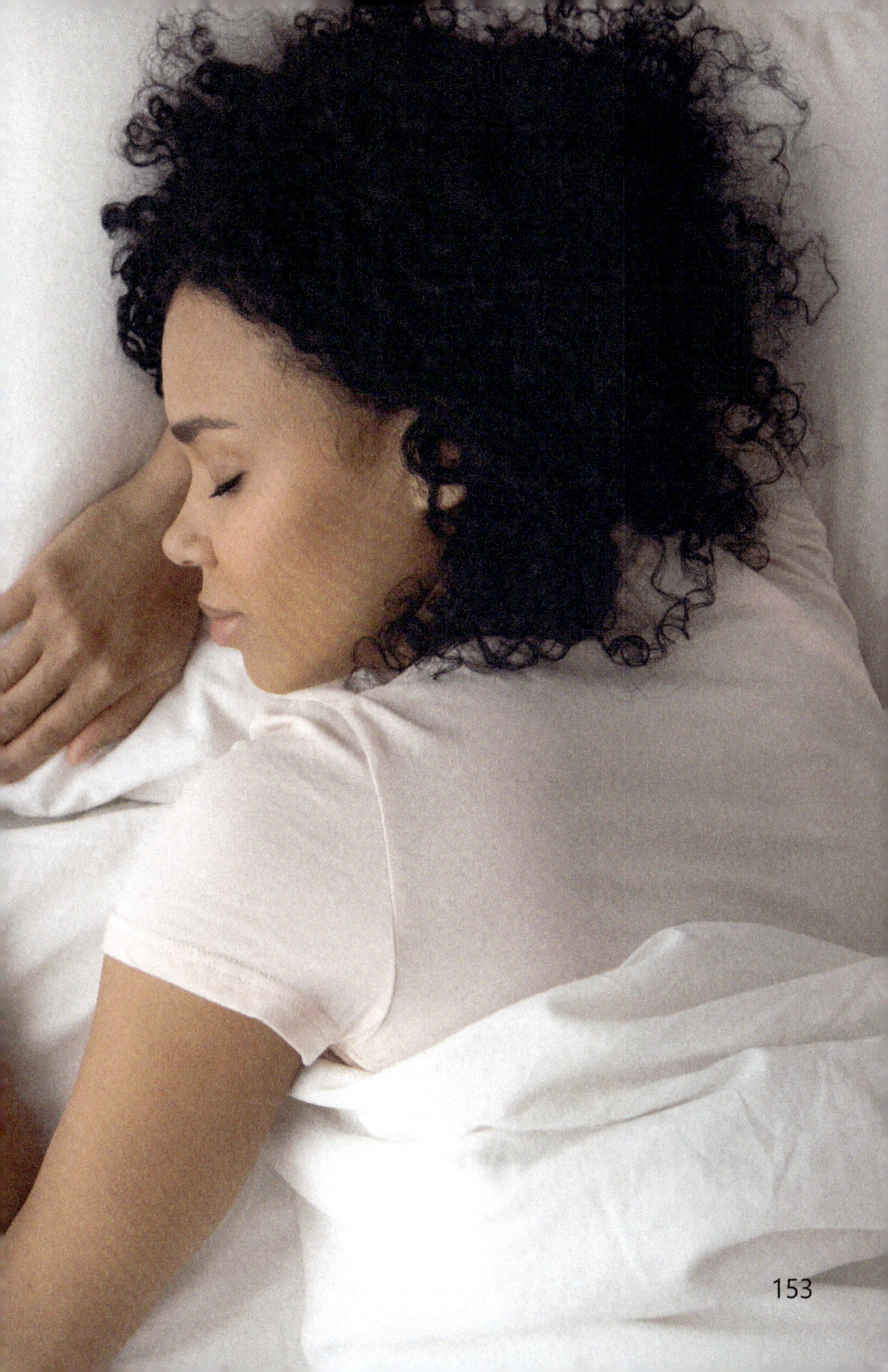

What Happens During Sleep

When you were a baby, you could sleep anywhere at any time. Sleep is one of the most natural things we do.

Like a child on a swing, the back and forth between wakefulness and sleep is a natural part of a person's rhythm of life.

Sleep isn't just one thing. There are several stages during which the body does different things to **consolidate, repair and regenerate**.

Sleep Stages

Light Sleep

This takes up most of the night. Your body processes memories and emotions and your metabolism regulates itself at this time.

Deep Sleep

The thinking parts of the brain are largely offline at this time. This is when the body repairs itself.

REM Sleep

During REM, your mind processes information and you may well dream. There is also some cellular rebuild at this time.

You go in and out of the sleep stages over the night.

Using a fitness tracker, such as Fitbit™, you can see your stages of sleep. You can also compare to benchmarks to see if you are getting enough.

By making changes in line with the 'Setting a Good Sleep Pattern' section of this book, you may find your sleep improves significantly.

Waking In The night?

Waking in the night is completely normal. Most people do.

Sometimes as we're going in and out of our sleep cycle, we just extend a little too much into awakeness.

This is nothing to bother about. Know that **just as you naturally came out of sleep, you can naturally drift back in**.

The following exercises may help relax you into sleep.

Getting Back To Sleep (Exercise 1)

Using your most tired, drowsy, boring voice, follow this pattern:

1. Close your eyes.
2. Say (in your head, using a really boring voice) "I am relaxing my _____"
3. Then, use your mind to feel that body part.
4. Imagine it relaxing twice as much as before. Breathe out slowly as you relax.

Do this for each body part in turn from head to toe.

e.g.

1. I am relaxing my forehead [feel, relax x2]
2. I am relaxing my eyebrows [feel, relax x2]
3. I am relaxing my eyes [feel, relax x2]
4. I am relaxing my ears [feel, relax x2]
5. I am relaxing my cheeks [feel, relax x2]
6. I am relaxing my nose [feel, relax x2]
7. I am relaxing my jaw [feel, relax x2]
8. I am relaxing my lips [feel, relax x2]
9. Carry on all the way down the body

Getting Back To Sleep (Exercise 2)

This is similar to an 'Elman Induction' hypnosis script, but works really well for relaxing yourself back into sleep. Read through a few times until you know it, then recall it if needed.

Exercise:

1. Take a long deep breath and close your eyes. Relax all the muscles around your eyes until they are so relaxed, they don't want to work.

2. Feel your eyelids getting relaxed and heavy until they feel like they can't open.

3. Test them and make sure they wont work. If you open your eyes, slowly close them and relax all the muscles around your eyes until they are too relaxed to work.

4. Start slowly counting backwards from 100. Each time you say a number, fall deeper into relaxation.

5. In between each number, slowly tell yourself any of the following words. You can use a different word each time:

    - Relaxing
    - Deeper
    - Drifting
    - Sleep

6. Make your count even slower as you go down the numbers.

159

Sleep Hypnosis

Hypnosis works really well for sleep.

If you **search for 'Paul McKenna Sleep Hypnosis' online**, you should find some **great sleep hypnosis recordings for free**!

Give them a few listens. If you're awake anyway, you may as well fill the time helping your body.

If you want more help, his book 'I Can Make You Sleep' is excellent.

There are many other hypnotists out there, but Paul is recognised as one of the greats.

Yoga Nidra

Yoga Nidra (yogic sleep) is a deeply relaxing body scan meditation that helps you get back to sleep.

If you have woken in the night, you may want to give it a try.

There are lots of free resources available.

If you **search 'Yoga Nidra' online or in good meditation apps**, you'll find plenty of options for gently getting back to sleep.

If you're sleeping with a partner, you can use earphones/earbuds to avoid waking them.

Setting A Good Sleep Pattern

1. Make your bed the comfiest, snuggliest place on earth!

2. Set an early alarm and get up! (Don't watch the clock in the night - the alarm is set, so you're safe). If you're feeling sluggish, consider having a cool/ cold shower when you wake.

3. Go to bed only when you're tired and ready.

4. If you're having trouble sleeping - don't nap. Else, don't nap after 2pm.

5. Get plenty of exercise (10K steps a day would be great!).

6. Finish eating at least 3 hours before bed.

7. Don't have caffeine after 2pm (ideally switch to decaf completely).

8. Ideally, cut out alcohol, or at least don't fill your tum near bedtime (reflux).

9. Avoid gritty dramas before bed (they get your adrenaline pumping). Consider light comedy instead.

10. Don't use any screen 1 hour before bed (blue light wakes you).

11. The bed is only for sleep and intimacy. No phones or tablets, no TV, no books!

12. Keep your bedroom dark at night.

13. Try to get a good temperature in the room (or at least in bed). Try to get a good airflow if possible.

14. Consider sleep hypnosis or 'yoga nidra' to help further relax into sleep.

15. If you wake in the night, try to relax back into sleep. Do the sleep exercises or meditation if needed. If you're still awake, get up and do something boring. Keep your wake time the same.

Confident, Organised & Positive

Failures of the past
are training for future success

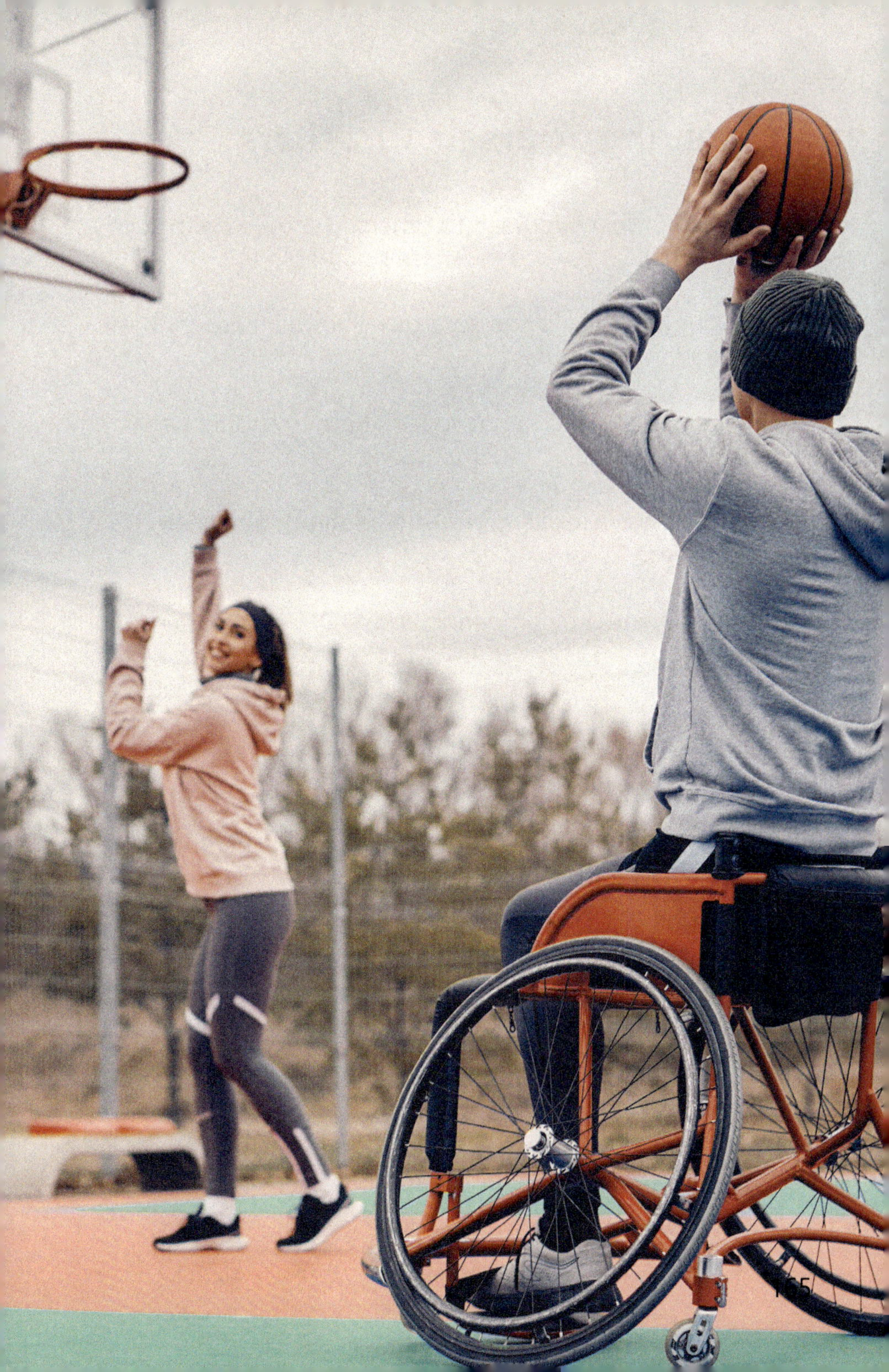

Comparing Yourself To Others

When you compare yourself to others, you do so with such bias as to make the whole exercise pointless.

Either your bias fails to see your own shortcomings, or more likely, you fail to see theirs.

It's a sure fire route to negative feelings and should be avoided at all costs!

The grass always looks greener when you look with envious eyes.

Notice when you are comparing and STOP!

Impressing Others

Nearly 2000 years ago, Marcus Aurelius wrote about the folly of trying to impress others.

Today, on social media, this is more evident than ever.

Think about the people you are trying to impress.

- **Are they really that impressive themselves?**
- **Are they worth your time and effort?**
- **Do they actually care about you?**

Incidentally, *not* putting something on social media gives you the chance to talk to friends about it and makes it completely new for them.

Mirror Neurons

Our brain is packed with 'mirror neurons'.

Mirror neurons naturally reflect what's around. They are an important part of how humans connect.

When someone smiles, the brains automatic response is to smile back. You also feel part of that joy (even if just a little).

The more you are around it, the more it takes hold. If you've been to a great carnival, festival or concert, you may have felt it very strongly.

Some things to consider:

- Remember that **happiness is contagious.**
- Spend more time around positive people.
- Watch positive programmes (swap the gritty dramas for comedy).
- **Promote yourself to 'Director of Happiness' and be the change for others** (which will then reflect back to you).

Smiling

When you smile, you can actively change how you feel.

Smiles are so interconnected to us, they actively stimulate the release of chemicals that make us more relaxed.

Exercise

1. Stand (or sit) in front of a mirror.

2. Smile. No matter how forced it is. Get a big cheesy grin going.

3. Hold it for 2 minutes! Whatever your mood, keep that smile going.

Do this for several days and see if you notice a difference.

Dealing With Difficult People

We all have to deal with difficult people - sometimes there's just no avoiding them (at work for example).

Take time to get to understand that person.

- Is there a reason why they behave in a certain way?
- What do they like or enjoy in life?
- Can you find anything in common?

Once you **understand more about that person**, you can do more to bring them on side.

You can't make friends with everyone, but any **move towards harmony** is a bonus for your day.

If you have a colleague that you feel is jealous of you, try asking for their advice (on something small to start). They are then part of the solution, so will have trouble to rally against it.

If you find a person to be uptight, but they light up when they talk about their kids - ask about their kids more. You may not be hugely interested, but by taking them to a happier place, your day will be happier too.

Conversation

After basic hygiene and respecting peoples' personal space, one of the key rules for conversation is: **expect acceptance**.

People are largely sociable and, at the time you meet, you are just a new friend in waiting.

People usually love to talk about themselves, so ask open questions (ones that can't be answered yes/no) and **find out what they enjoy**.

If they are talking about something that fills them with happy feelings, that will rub off to an association with you. You might find something in common too.

Be patient. If you are a fast talker and they are slow, don't interrupt. Slow down and **match their pace**. If you're the slower one, try increasing your pace a little.

If they aren't sociable (or they don't fill you with joy), politely move on. There are eight billion other people to try.

Be Happy With Who You Are

Everyone has something they would change about themselves.

Smarter, more attractive, bigger bum, smaller bum, the list goes on.

The only thing ever holding you back is your mind.

People of all shapes and size find love. People with very different abilities find success.

Sometimes, the thing you'd change actually helps you stand out from the crowd.

Use Your Best Stuff

Why buy something, then not use it?

You bought it because you like it, right?

Say you have a nice tea set.

If you store it away and only get it out twice a year, the joy you get is quite limited. If you live another 60 years, you've had just 120 uses.

But, if you use that tea set every day (and are careful!), **you could get 1000's of days filled with moments of joy**.

It may pick up a chip or two, but then that becomes part of the beauty and its story.

Enjoy Being Consistently Inconsistent

Things take time. You can't always be at your best.

Sometimes we're happy, sometimes we aren't. Sometimes we're filled with energy, other times we just want to hide under the duvet!

It's important to understand that changes in energy levels and capabilities are completely normal.

Be grateful of the good times and accepting of the bad.

Everyone drops the ball every now and then. Anyone who doesn't allow you that doesn't truly care for you.

When something bad has happened, but doesn't really matter, think of the term 'oh well'. Accept it for what it is and move on.

The Little Things Add Up

How much time do you give someone (or something) without distraction?

What if you gave something your full attention for just a short period?

For example: If you are a parent, what if you spent 15 minutes a day with your child where you only focussed on them. No phones, cooking or other distractions.

On it's own, that doesn't seem like much, but let's see how it builds up:

Time	Total
1 day	15 mins
1 week	1.75 hours
1 month	7.5 hours
1 year	3.8 days (solid)
5 years	19 days (solid)
18 years	68.5 days (solid)

How much would you learn? How much more could you bond?

This can work with all sorts of things.

If you don't have big blocks of time, could you manage lots of little times?

Break It Down

Making a long term goal, or having a long term project can feel like a real trudge through the mud.

The problem comes from having a target so far away.

There's no achievement for ages, then you get to the end and you're relieved it's over.

This graph shows a traditional approach. Doesn't look much fun, does it?

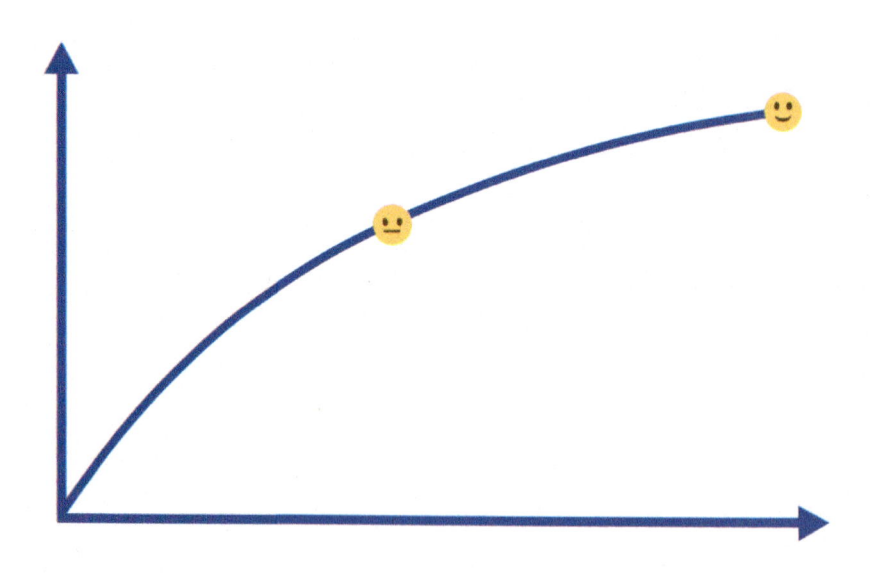

By **breaking down big goals into lots of little goals** and, importantly, **celebrating each 'win',** you will get **much more enjoyment** out of the process.

As a result, you might get there quicker too!

Does this way look more fun to you?

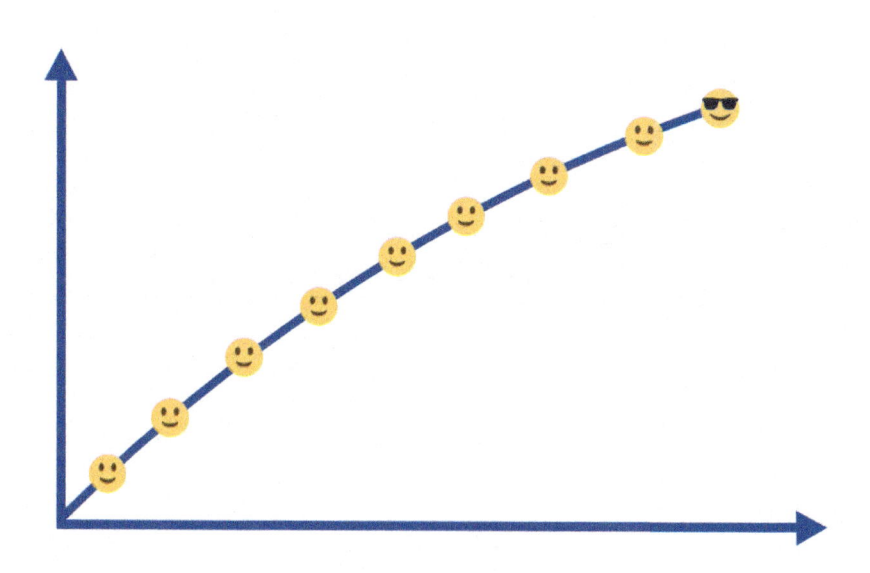

The Eisenhower Matrix

If you need help with prioritisation, the Eisenhower Matrix is worth considering.

Remember that for most tasks 'close enough is good enough!'.

1. Urgent And Important	2. Important, But Not Urgent
Do these first!	These impact your life, health or career. This includes hobbies! Do these second!
3. Urgent, But Not Important	4. Not Important, Not Urgent
Delegate this stuff if possible and don't let someone else's priorities overtake your second column. Do these third.	Avoid Completely. Either priorities will change, or they don't really need doing.

Challenge Self-Imposed Deadlines

Yes - there are times when deadlines matter, but most of the time, they don't.

For example - 'I need to do the washing today':

- **Do you *need* to?**
- **Must it be *today*?**

Sometimes, it's good to get ahead, as long as you rest when you're done.

Quite often, these self-imposed deadlines are arbitrary and have no real reason other than having a bee in your bonnet!

It's great to be motivated but, by going a little easier on yourself with stuff that doesn't matter, you can make life much less stressful.

Notice Every Little Win

Every time something goes right, actively notice it.

It doesn't have to be big or important.

- Had an ice cream all to yourself - WIN!
- Got the last sandwich in the shop - WIN!
- Got a delivery on the expected delivery date - WIN!

Get used to winning and enjoy it.

The more you notice the wins, the more your **positivity builds**.

As your positivity builds, you become more open to opportunities and, sooner or later, those opportunities will become bigger wins.

Danish Work Culture

Denmark consistently ranks as one of the happiest countries in the world.

Among many great habits, one of particular note is that of work.

In a Danish company, time is allowed for cakes and socialising. It is normal to finish bang on time.

Importantly, if you are working overtime, you are likely to be questioned over your time management skills!

When you leave your workplace, you can stop working.

Turn off any phone notifications. Emails can wait.

If it's not paid work time, it's your time to do what you enjoy. It's as if your workplace doesn't even exist.

Power Poses For Confidence

1. Pick one of the poses shown in the images below - 'The Superhero', or 'The Winner'. Imagine the feeling that goes with that pose. Really get into it.

2. Hold that pose for two minutes.

3. Feel the energy and positivity continue inside you as you go about your day.

Good Posture

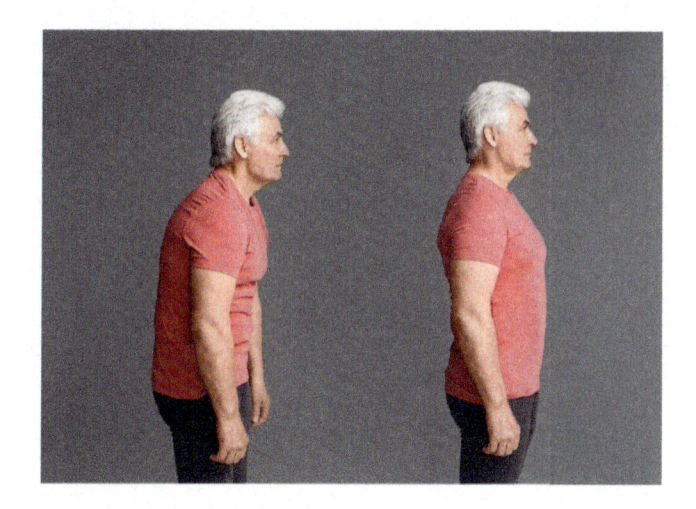

Look at the picture above.

On the left is bad posture. Shoulders hunched, crease in the neck. How does this man look? Does he look strong and confident?

Now, look at the posture on the right. Shoulders back, head held high (imagine a string holding up the crown of his head), weight evenly distributed. How does he look now? Is it likely he feels stronger and more confident?

Good posture is important whether standing or sitting.

As well as physical benefits such as improved balance and better energy flows, good posture has been shown to boost self esteem and reduce stress and anxiety.

It's a really simple change that can make a big difference to how you feel.

Taking The Compliment

We can better embrace positive living in the way we handle compliments.

When someone says thank you, or mentions something good you've done, there is a tendency to deflect it.

You might say "Oh, it was nothing", or tell them how it nearly didn't happen.

Instead, just **accept the compliment** and say "Thank you", or "You're welcome".

Internally, **congratulate yourself** on a job well done.

Story Telling

When you tell a story, you don't need to include the whole story.

You had a great walk, but there was some litter on the ground.

You went to see a friend, but the train was late and really hot.

When you add these bits of **negativity, you reduce the pleasure in your own memories** of the event.

By telling a story more positively, you are feeding your own imagination. You can relive the event in a more energising way for yourself as well as those you are talking to.

What Would Your Hero Do?

If you are stuck on a problem, a simple question to ask might be - what would my hero do?

It doesn't have to be a comic book superhero, just someone who would be really good in that situation.

It could be a friend, colleague, or someone on TV/ online.

In fact, if you can't think of anyone, it can be someone you imagine being great at it.

By taking yourself out of the picture and 'having someone else look at it', you can open your mind to more creative ideas.

Getting What You Want From Life

When you're trying to figure out what to do to get what you want from life, try the following exercise. It's a form of 'The Miracle Question'.

1. Imagine - What would your perfect future look like?

Take time to relax. Picture the scene. What would it look like? How would it sound? How would it feel? What is happening around you? Imagine all the details you can. How would a friend know you are in this perfect state?

When you've done this and are really enjoying it, make the colours bolder and brighter, the smells stronger and anything you touch fizz with positive energy that flows into you.

2. Now, ask yourself - What changes would have had to have happened for you to get there?

If the changes are big, how could you break them down? What are the little goals on the way? What are your next steps in making them happen?

Have Fun

A really key part of a happier future is simply to have more fun!

Finding wholesome, non-screen-based fun will make a world of difference to your life.

Maybe go swimming, play board games, start a new class?

Find what you enjoy and do more of it. If you feel you don't have time, can you cut something out to make time? If not, can you find ways of adding fun to what you're already doing?

The power of clean fun really cannot be overstated. It's magic!

You need it. You deserve it.

Have More Fun!

Remember, fun is anywhere you make it.

Think of things you can do whatever your circumstance. All you need is a brain and you're good to go.

- Make your own puns and plays on words. Think rhymes, opposites, or just taking a thought on a fun journey.

- Be silly for the fun of it.

- Try being cheeky (with the right people).

- Try new things and give it your all. If you try 'jungle drumming', drum like you're trying to wake the entire world. If it's rubbish, laugh about how rubbish it was. If you loved it, make more of those feelings.

Effortless Confidence

Read through this exercise then take some time to try it.

1. Close your eyes.

2. Imagine you are at an upcoming event. See what you would see, hear what you would hear and feel what you would feel.

3. Notice your posture and, if needed, change it to something that feels confident. You're in a relaxed alert state, ready for anything.

4. Run through scenarios that might occur at the event. Whatever happens, imagine handling it with calmness and confidence. You've got this.

5. Notice how confident you sound as you talk to those around you.

6. Imagine every movement you make doubles your energy and confidence. Move and feel your energy increase.

7. Take time to revel in this feeling. Feel yourself exuding energy and light.

8. When you are ready, slowly come back to the room, taking all those good feelings with you wherever you go.

191

Further Reading

Further Reading

There are so many great books out there. It's hard to narrow down just a few to go on with. Keeping easy reading in mind, here are a few of our favourites:

- **Freedom From Anxiety** - Paul McKenna

- **Get The Life You Love NOW** - Phil Parker (creator of The Lightning Process)

- **Practicing The Power Of Now** - Ekhart Tolle

- **I Can Make You Sleep** - Paul McKenna

- **Mindfulness** - Prof. Mark Williams/ Dr. Danny Penman

- **Super Coach/ The Inside-Out Revolution** - M. Neill

- **The Daily Stoic** - Ryan Holiday and Stephen Hanselman

- **The Path** - Prof. Michael Puett and Christine Gross-Loh

Finish Fast?

There was no right or wrong way to read this book.

If it took a while, great. If you rumbled through in no time, that's great too.

If you skipped the exercises, you might want to go back and try a few. They really make a difference.

Remember:

You are both the farmer and the fruit of the farm.

Keep sowing the seeds and looking after the crop. The benefits will be limitless!

Keep in mind that this book is always here for you. **Keep it and flick back through once in a while.**

You might pick up something you missed before.

Wishing you good health, harmony and happiness.

Ann-Marie and Justin

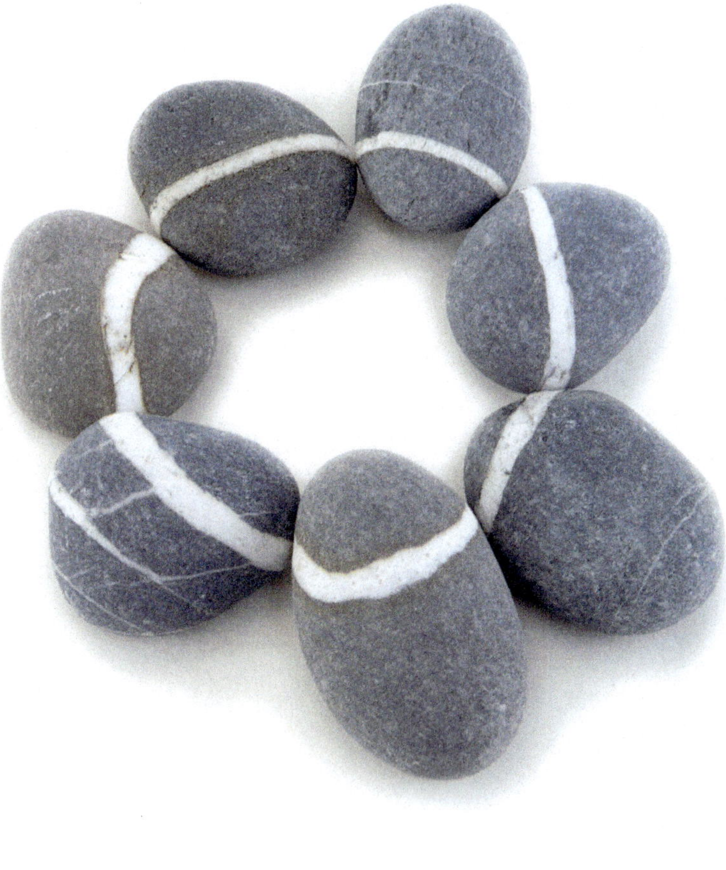

Printed in Great Britain
by Amazon